# GET
## PROMOTED

# GET
## *PROMOTED*

**WHAT YOU'RE *REALLY* MISSING AT WORK
THAT'S HOLDING YOU BACK**

*MICHAEL
WENDEROTH*

Michael Wenderoth
 michael@changwenderoth.com
https://changwenderoth.com

Get Promoted, Michael Wenderoth—1st ed. ISBN: 978-1-955242-21-9

# PRAISE FOR GET PROMOTED

"*Get Promoted* is a must-read for anyone who wants to accelerate their career. Michael breaks down decades of research (so you don't have to) and shows you exactly how to land your next role, win your next raise, and get big things done at work!"

—Dorie Clark, Top 50 Business Thinkers in the World (Thinkers50), Author WSJ Bestseller *The Long Game*

---

"*Get Promoted* does not have a lot of feel-good advice. But if you look critically at what Michael suggests — and put it in practice - you will move the needle on your career and your initiatives, and enhance your leadership profile. Michael is a serious, fresh voice who holds a consolidated experience as coach and executive trainer in very diverse environments. His book is going to help a lot of people."

—Santiago Iñiguez de Onzoño, President IE University, recognised influencer in global higher education and Vice-Chairman of Headspring (owned by the Financial Times and IE Business School)

---

"Michael Wenderoth has coached in the online version of my power class since it began, helping participants to surmount their own self-created obstacles and become more powerful and successful. This well-written, engaging book presents his tips and lessons in a concise and practical fashion that will help readers to turn knowledge about power and organizational realities into effective actions."

—Jeffrey Pfeffer, Professor at Stanford's Graduate School of Business and author of *7 Rules of Power*

---

"Finally, a leadership book that skips generalities and happy talk and gets to the heart of what really matters for success – relationships, power dynamics and how you manage them. For those of you frustrated that your great ideas and hard work aren't paying off, Michael's book explains why and what to do about it. Mandatory reading."

—Alisia Gill, Chief People Officer at EmpiRx Health

---

"Read the Introduction and Chapter 3 and you'll see the passion, commitment and deep thinking Michael brings to his coaching clients. It's never too late to *Get Promoted* — although I wish I had this book this 20 years ago!"

—Keshav Pitani, VP of R&D, Scientific Games

"This is an excellent book, creatively written and organized, replete with practical and actionable strategies for advancing your career. After reading *Get Promoted* you'll have the understanding and the tools to focus on what matters most."

—Robert Goodwin, Retired Dean of the Graduate School and Professor, University of Maryland Global Campus, and Former EVP and General Counsel, Chindex International. Named Who's Who in America and Who's Who in the Law. Former member, U.S. Federal Senior Executive Service.

---

"We all need to build power in our lives and in our communities, and Michael breaks down how you do that. Whether you are trying to get promoted, make the system better, or help others, *Get Promoted* is broadly applicable in showing how this can be done. I'm recommending this to current, aspiring and future leaders I work with, at all levels."

—Virginia Tan, Founding Partner, Teja Ventures; Co-Founder, She Loves Tech; Founder, Lean In China; Asia 21 Leader Class of 2022, The Peak Power List 2021

---

"Sadly, the age-old advice of "work hard, get ahead" can take you only so far. *Get Promoted* shines a light on factors that can unwittingly derail your success, and offers a step-by-step action plan that will put you in the driver's seat to take charge of your career advancement."

—Marie Mookini, PhD. Former Director of the Sloan Master's Program and Director of MBA Admissions, Stanford Graduate School of Business.

---

"I've developed and coached thousands of executives and helped them become good bosses and great leaders. Michael's book can help with this journey. He highlights the often overlooked need to proactively influence your career through the mastery and balance of Power & Politics. Michael's ideas and framework helps ensure more of the RIGHT PEOPLE become powerful leaders."

—Dr. Gary McGrath, CEO Statarius

"For too long, highly competent and ethical individuals have not thought deeply about how to put themselves into a position to have the impact they deserve. Michael Wenderoth has adroitly highlighted the importance not only of an individual's performance but of proactively creating and executing a personal strategy to produce the right results."

—David Thrower, Chief Commercial Officer, uLab Systems and former CEO at Baronova, Asante and InSound Medical.

"I've seen too many amazingly talented executives stall out or get derailed— right when they should be rising and coming into their own. Read *Get Promoted* so that doesn't happen to you!"

—Rebecca Zucker, Founding Partner at Next Step Partners, Executive Coach, *Harvard Business Review* Contributor & MG100 Coach.

"Why would a medical doctor – or any professional – be interested in a book on getting promoted, on power? Because our effectiveness and success is driven heavily by our ability to influence others – be that getting the best out of our team, leading critical transformations in our organizations, or shaping the future of our industry. Michael's book will help you become more strategic, deliberate and successful at whatever you seek to do."

—Dr. Bill G. Kortesis, MD, FACS. Aesthetic & MedTech Venture Advisor; Owner & Managing Partner of H/K/B Cosmetic Surgery; America's Best Plastic Surgeons 2021 list (Newsweek)

---

"My coaching and books are focused on the practical – getting busy executives where they want to go. *Get Promoted* does all of that, and more. This provocative and valuable guide will accelerate your ascent."

— L. Bonita Patterson, Founder and CEO Polaris Consulting Group, Author and Executive Coach

---

"As one of the leading recruitment organizations in the U.S., we know that top talent wants to make a big impact and rise fast. Michael provides a clear and actionable guide to what it takes to ascend. This is THE book for nice guys who don't want to finish last and I consider it mandatory reading for all aspiring leaders."

—Keith Wolf, Managing Director at Murray Resources and CEO at ResumeSpice (Top recruiter in Texas and 6x Inc. 5000 Fastest-Growing Company Award-winner)

---

"Guanxi and the power of networks is alive and well, everywhere. Understand how the game is played if you wish to win at it — or seek to change it. You'll never look at your organization quite the same again."

—Camiel Gielkens, CEO at Schouten & Nelissen

---

"Navigating the corporate world can be challenging. As an Asian American woman taught to work hard, and keep your head down, I found that the key principles outlined here are paramount and critical to embrace in order to break through multiple ceilings. This playbook breaks it down so simply and practically and had I known these principles earlier, my career would have had a smoother trajectory!"

—Lisa Wang, Managing Director, Head of Marketing & Communications, Asia Pacific, PineBridge Investments

---

"I am fond of a Chinese proverb with a twist: "The journey of a thousand miles begins with a single step — in the right direction." *Get Promoted* will expand your toolkit, challenge those societal norms, and get you thinking about what will truly accelerate your impact. A deeply thought-provoking read that speaks truth to power, is deeply inclusive in its architecture, and lays out a pragmatic career playbook for those seeking to not only survive but also thrive in a friction-free and reputation economy."

—Leesa Soulodre, General Partner R3i Ventures; Partner SheLovesTech, Adjunct Singapore Management University.

"Michael is one of the executive world's most successful coaches because he seamlessly combines unparalleled common sense, practical know-how, and academic research. Whether you're just starting your career or a decade into your corporate journey, you need to read this book. If you diligently use the strategies inside, I wouldn't be surprised if you find yourself with a new title or substantial bonus in the not so distant future."

—Jason Hreha, Founder and CEO Persona,
former Global Head of Behavioral Science at Walmart

---

"This is an extraordinary book. One of my great frustrations as an Executive Education Professor is seeing the bad guys win. You may be a team player, who does not discriminate or take credit for the work of others – but do not assume that everyone else is the same! Just because some people use power for evil does not mean that you can not use it for good. One of the values of IE Business School is diversity. What reading Michael's book has done is made me realise that we have to move beyond just preaching the value of diversity and expecting that the world will self correct itself. No. We have to provide the tools in the classroom so that, irrespective of your background, missing out on promotions and awards becomes no one's fault except your own."

—Professor Joe Haslam, Executive Director, Owners Scaleup
Program, IE Business School (Madrid, Spain)

"Having worked closely with Michael in the past as a Coach at Stanford Business School, I can tell you he calls it as he sees it and is spot on. For everyone who shies away from influence, power and office politics, you must read *Get Promoted*. Michael's playbook will help you confront the real barrier that's holding you back: yourself."

—Kevin Williams, MBA (Stanford),
Doctorate (USC), and global leader at LinkedIn

---

"Michael has always looked at things differently. In *Get Promoted*, he weighs insightfully into the topic everyone shies away from: power and office politics. As a COO, whose job is to get stuff done, I can tell you that people ought to read this book – at the start of their careers, again in the middle – and yet again when they reach the highest ranks."

—James Liu, Entrepreneur, Internet Executive and Investor. COO and Executive Director, Renren Inc (formerly Oak Pacific Interactive)

---

"This book reveals the hidden truth in the Chinese expression, "干活不由东累死也无功" "Working hard you can't help but grow exhausted and find it of no use." The structure of a modern enterprise is so complex – and changing – that people often don't know who the real boss is: the bosses of their boss, someone sitting in the C-SUITE or the chairman who can only show his face occasionally on video. To help get focus, read *Get Promoted*!"

—Sylvia Pan, GM Beijing United Hospitals and Clinics

"My coaching practice specializes in mastering interpersonal skills and building a career of meaning and impact. Many people perceive power and politics to be Machiavellian and may think that Michael and I are on "opposite ends" of the coaching spectrum. Nothing could be farther from the truth. Michael shows you why power is so critical and provides a thoughtful guide that will encourage you to be more strategic about what you do ... For anyone planning their next career moves, read *Get Promoted*!"

—Agnes Le, Executive Coach & Career Strategist; former Director of Career Development at Stanford Graduate School of Business.

www.agnesle.com

---

"Michael's coaching and support helped me be attentive to power and politics with pragmatism… and with his book, he is going to help you too... an invaluable guide that will help you see problems as opportunities… "

—Eduardo Itar Kimura, Executive Director, Head of Technology and Transformation at Voiter Bank (São Paulo, Brazil); former Partner at PriceWaterhouseCoopers (PwC), and Senior Executive at IBM, Accenture and Microsoft.

"Self-promotion is a sharp instrument. You may have avoided it or have tried but hurt yourself. You may believe that your results speak for themselves, and soon they will speak for you. You may struggle at the bottom of a hierarchy, on the way up or towards opportunities in another country or sector. In either case, Michael's book is the manual to turn your hard work into influence."

—Gabor Holch, East-West Leadership coach, consultant & keynote speaker

"In *Get Promoted*, Michael Wenderoth lays out the uncomfortable truths about what it REALLY takes to move up in today's organizations. Working alongside Michael at Stanford Business School, I've seen him repeatedly share these uncomfortable (yet necessary) truths to help executives move ahead in their careers. True to Michael's style, *Get Promoted* provides a clear, actionable playbook that will help you identify and then move beyond what's holding YOU back so you can get to your next level."

—Inbal Demri, PhD, CEO of Q Factor Consulting.

"Michael's straight-forward insights are critical to understanding how the world of work actually functions. Politics and power are uncomfortable topics that need to be addressed head-on. Our idealistic students and alumni will benefit from utilizing the practical strategies to create their success stories across the globe."

—RJ Holmes-Leopold, Director of the Career Center, Carleton College

"This should be mandatory reading in business schools. It's critical to be able to evaluate the landscape you are working in. Michael's book will help you incorporate reality into your operating model at work, and help you make the right choices for your next move. "

—Scott Wambolt, CEO, Dark Horse Intelligence

---

"The topics in this book are viewed very negatively by Chinese people. Michael's book unpacks the hard truth, but provides a strategic map and tactical action plan – which have encouraged me to re-examine my career path and influence assets. Follow this playbook and you can harvest how to achieve your career goal in a strategic and focused way."

—Wish Wang, CEO A-Ha Consulting and online influencer
(Shanghai, China)

---

"The concrete examples and clear advice will help you embrace reality and learn how the system works. The special insights devoted to challenges faced by women and people of color in the workplace are especially useful. This book will help you set – but more importantly accomplish – your goals by understanding how to influence."

—Kimberly Betz, Career Center Director, top ranked national
universities and colleges

"*Get Promoted* unlocks critical and widely misunderstood keys to creating impact in your career: owning your power and ethically wielding influence. It's a captivating read that translates well-researched theories into very real practice!"

—Rebecca Lovell, CEO Denali Founder Consulting; Chair of the Board of Directors, Center for American Entrepreneurship

---

"I went from a small prototype of fermenting Cacao in Acacia wooden boxes in a village in the South of Vietnam to a proposal of a 4.5 billion dollar Green Bond to the World Bank, thus pushing for re-inventing a troublesome supply chain at the global level. The amount of influence needed to achieve any disruptive strategy is enormous and can't be achieved without understanding the basic rules of the Power game. Michael's coaching was essential in helping me and my team to play that game literally by the rules – allowing us to develop our influence at levels we did not think were possible."

—Gricha Safarian, Founder CACAO-TRACE; Shareholder and Managing Director, Puratos Grand-Place Indochina; Impact Investor

---

"Michael has launched innovative products and businesses by challenging the status quo and conventional wisdom. In *Get Promoted*, he challenges your cherished beliefs, and gives you the hard and soft skills needed to manage in any business environment."

—Brent Irvin, Vice President and General Counsel at Tencent; Head of Tencent America

# CLIENT TESTIMONIALS

The most rewarding part of what I do is helping my clients succeed.

Here is how they describe the process and insights that you will read about. (Names and potentially identifying details have been changed).

> *"I was emotionally tied up with the ideas of "right vs wrong" instead of looking at it objectively and doing the optimal things I can do. Working through the power map and the relative importance of the people helped clarify to me that my priorities were all up-side-down. I was haggling over minor things I have no control over and ignoring things I could control. Going over the important people and how they can help me increase my influence was an eye-opener. This helped me a great deal… It is, indeed, the foundation for many things I did afterwards and continue to do now."*
>
> *- Ben, Director (now VP) of R&D, global software company*

> *"If more people were less theoretical and had a real world street level understanding of how the business world really worked, they would do much better. That was most helpful working with Michael… Play the game or get played! I'm*

*now 300% happier in my day to day life. I would not have gotten there had I not gone through the process. ."*

*- Ana, SVP, insurance industry*

*"I benefited most from the candor. This was telling it like it is, in a way that fosters growth. You helped put me in a position to see important things for myself through the critical thinking exercises. As a direct result of the coaching, I got the highest rating for that year leading to financial rewards and a new lease of life to an otherwise stalled career."*

*- Vishant, Sr. Director, internet leader*

*"This encouraged me to play a bigger game and that what I have to offer already is very compelling in the marketplace— no need to keep waiting to get the right experience or have the perfect insight."*

*- Elena, Head of HR, digital advertising agency*

*"I did not see an avenue for growth. I did not have a boss who saw a path for growth for me. And from a cultural perspective, I had to navigate with people who did not look like me... It was hard to be heard... This process totally flipped the script, and we worked through the important cultural challenges I faced. My professional circle has grown, and the blunt reality made me realize that nothing changes if nothing changes. I tapped into those real accelerators and that has made a massive difference."*

*- Marta, Senior Director, computer industry*

*"I was lacking a clear and schematic understanding of what was happening and the strategy to counter it. I decreased the dramatization of some emotional issues and started to*

*think more in tactical terms depending on the people I was
dealing with."*

> *- Greg, General Manager, luxury goods retailer*

*"I got out of my own way (stopped sabotaging myself),
becoming more productive and focused, and was able to take
smart risks as small steps (experiment more). That led to
getting my dream job in innovation, which has continued,
getting me speaking roles, industry association positions,
which have led to even more opportunities."*

> *- Mark, Sr. Director of Innovation, global
> pharmaceutical company*

*"Because of the work you did, one of my employees was able
to secure a key role, one she was previously told by many
she was not qualified to hold. As her boss, I was thrilled you
used a structured, proven approach that produces consistent,
sustained results."*

> *- Tina, Sr. Director, global tech company*

*"The process gave me a totally new perspective on the
workplace. Before working with you, I saw everything from a
surface point of view. After working with you, I understood
the churning and hidden dynamics at play at work. I focused
on one key action or key behavior at a time, and that made
all the difference. I also realized what was getting in the way
was me."*

> *- Alex, VP, investment bank*

*"I got promoted! At the time I thought it was too aggressive.
I am not sure I would have advocated for myself had I not
gone through this process. It made me come to terms with the*

*concept that "what got me here isn't going to get me there" as I have come to a critical point in my career. I was and still am on the upward trajectory, but I was seeing myself get in my own way—this lit a fire underneath me to make the ask for more resources, and to my amazement, it happened in a much faster timeframe than expected. My undercutting language has considerably decreased (and is a continued work in progress), and I am more aware of my presence and how intentional I need to be with it. I've made great additions to my network and a sharpened focus that will benefit me for years to come."*

*- Pranati, Senior Manager, e-commerce leader*

*"I recently got promoted and continue to benefit from the tools. I had an "a-ha" moment while thinking about my power map again recently, which helped me fill a business and personal need of a mentor, which turned him into a sponsor. That information (what he needs) has been sitting there in front of me for months, but it took the power map for me to realize how I should be using that to my advantage. It's a fantastic tool. I also didn't really appreciate how useful many resources are, and I look at activities in a new way— like taking a strategic seat on certain committees, which increased my visibility and helped my network. In the past I would have ignored that and focused on delivering results. I have started to actively participate in those because in some instances, they do provide a direct line to senior management that I otherwise would not have."*

*- Rob, GM, telecom industry*

*"As a result of being more strategic, I was given more responsibilities and some projects that have an enterprise-wide reach, which I have been both busy with and excited about. Additionally, after speaking with my manager and the leadership team about my career goals, I convinced them to finance an online HR data analytics course, which has further benefited me. This opened up my mind and my career path… They didn't teach this stuff in my school or at my company. Thank you!"*

*- Raj, Associate, consulting firm*

*"Being strategic and assessing the landscape, I realized the odds were not good. I normally would have stuck it out, gotten frustrated. This helped me identify the truth faster and take actions that quickly set me up for another great opportunity (new job!) before I left. An accurate read of the power dynamics was critical and is already helping me here at my new organization."*

*- Tanya, Division Lead, tech company*

# DEDICATION

*To Y-poh, Y-gon, Grandmom and Grandpop for showing me what hard work and persistence looks like.*

*To Mom for your dogged intensity, and to Dad for your thoughtful reflection.*

*To Victoria, mi media naranja. Without your support, this book and what we have together would not be possible. Te quiero mucho.*

*To Miguel and Victoria, work hard, be curious—but build power.*

# GET PROMOTED

What you're *really* missing at work that's holding you back

# CONTENTS

"活到老，学到老"
Huo dao lao, xue dao lao
(Never stop learning)
– Chinese idiom


"If you only read the books that everyone else is reading,
you can only think what everyone else is thinking."

– Haruki Murakami

# BEGINNINGS
## Clearing the Fog

"Alter any early event, ever so slightly and without apparent importance at the time, and evolution cascades into a radically different channel."

- Stephen Jay Gould

# INTRODUCTION

# The Painful Backstory

I remember the moment like yesterday.

Matt, a close friend, called me on the phone. Silence. Then his voice shook. He had been fired.

Matt (not his real name) had been, and still is, part of a small group of people that I deeply admire.[1] He was off-the-charts smart, incredibly hardworking, highly ethical, personable and, most of all, someone who cared deeply about other people. He was the kind of guy you wanted on your team— or leading your team. Many of us saw him destined for the C-Suite.

"I'm so angry and upset. I feel like the rug got pulled out from under me."

Over the next several months, Matt got bitter and depressed, and I could see him taking out his frustrations at home.

---

[1]   Name and identifying details changed. All examples in this book are based on my clients and executives I have worked with, unless otherwise stated.

The news was totally shocking. He had given everything to that company and had risen rapidly and deservingly to a fairly senior role before being unceremoniously dumped.

I got angry too: *How could such a bad thing happen to such a good person?*

Over the next decade, as I progressed through my corporate career, I saw this same story—bad things happening to great people—play out in places I worked and to classmates from college and business school.

The ones I *expected* to rise to the top, were often stalling, hitting ceilings, getting derailed—or were increasingly frustrated that they weren't able to make an impact or ascend.

Meanwhile, I was surprised by many that *were getting ahead*. They were not always the smartest or hardest workers nor had the deepest domain knowledge. But they had ambition and confidence, often what felt like overly high opinions of themselves. Many presented themselves extremely well, but most of all, they all had an uncanny way of being in the right place or around the right project and people. Even average performance results did not seem to impede their ascent.

I felt a massive disconnect.

Those, like Matt, who had followed the common career and leadership advice—to work hard, be humble and authentic, and be a team player—were actually *not faring the best*. In fact, they were frustrated that they weren't better recognized and rewarded.

Those who seemed to operate by a different playbook—or in more than a few cases, were aggressive, self-promoting narcissists—were having a field day. They were getting ahead with promotions, outsized bonuses, plum assignments, and fantastic job offers.

*This felt so unfair!*

I'm a bit of a geek and skeptical of slick motivational speakers, so I turned to see if academic research could explain what was going on.

That only made things more puzzling.

There was amazing work—literally decades of it—that explained why this second group was getting ahead. Yet I had never been exposed to much of it. Matt and people in the first group must have missed this important message too.

Or maybe we had gotten the message but had rejected it? After all, the second group often acts in ways that repel us. They "used" influential relationships, could come across as aggressive or bossy, they took credit shamelessly. They didn't always play nice or fair and seldom acted like self-effacing "servant leaders". When they did get to the top or share their stories, however, they talked a great game about being a humble, team player—but that was hardly how they *really* rose or operated.

The second group, through savvy political skills, used strategies to build and wield power that got them things they wanted.

The deeper, upsetting fact is that there is substantial evidence that people like Matt—thoughtful leaders who listen, are inclusive, admit when they don't know—can be better leaders. Their organizations perform better than those of the swashbuckling narcissists.

The problem: the thoughtful first group, the Matts, were *not getting to positions of greatest influence or leadership*. Putting titles and positions aside, they often weren't even in the game, where they could make the greatest impact. The Matts were getting sidelined.

The hard reality was a cold slap in the face. To get ahead, did the Matts need to do the same things as the second group or become those people?

Then it dawned on me that I was looking at this in the wrong way.

We have very negative feelings about the second group. But take, for example, their ability to network, and build relationships with influential people. There is nothing inherently evil about that. Having a strong tie with a key decision maker or knowing vital people across the organization makes it a lot easier to discover valuable information and get things done.

Maybe the second group really *was skilled and competent?* Could we learn from them?

I couldn't help but reflect on my own career and the focus my Chinese immigrant grandparents had ingrained in me: "Keep your head down, do great work, and you will get rewarded." That *had* gotten me pretty far. But could I have risen higher—had more impact—had I been exposed earlier to this "hard reality"? And as I tracked the careers of people who had worked for me, I consistently saw the "smart, head down hard workers" hit ceilings.

More importantly, I was deeply curious: Could the Matts learn, even embrace "political" behaviors and strategies to build power, which would help them get ahead—*without becoming* the toxic, flashy leaders, the ones that organizations sadly often got?

Could power and politics be harnessed for "good"?

When I became an executive coach years later, I acted on this passion and insight. I began to help executives re-examine their assumptions about power, politics, and authenticity. At the very least, I would help executives build the skills and awareness, so they would never experience the pain of getting stalled and frustrated, or derailed, like Matt. At the very best, harnessing new skills would amplify their impact and help them ascend to the highest levels or break glass ceilings—imposed by those around them, but more often by themselves—that were holding them back.

I challenge executives to confront what they are *really missing*, to discover the "hard truths" playbook they were never given. But we go beyond awareness. As an executive coach, my job is to help my clients not just discover new insights but apply them to their situation. Learning and applying is what gets results.

To date, I have helped thousands of diverse, global executives through my 1-1 coaching, speaking, and workshops. I'm proud of the results: My clients have gained valuable new perspectives and skills that have made them more effective leaders. They have been promoted, received outsized bonuses and raises, launched major transformations—and continue to be approached for highly coveted roles, long after working with me.

This book provides the top insights, strategies, and tools presented in a 3-step framework—the Rock, the Map, and the Snowball—that has helped them through their journeys.

It can help you, too, if you give it a chance.

As Gloria Steinem said, *"The truth will set you free, but first it will really piss you off."* My book is not for everyone. It will challenge much of the prevailing career and leadership advice, most of which is feel-good nonsense and won't help you.

If you are stuck, seek the extra edge, or tired of advice that isn't connected to reality, this is your "hard truth" playbook. If you are open and ready to be challenged—and willing to take important steps to address what you are *really* missing that's holding you back—buckle up, and let's begin.

Michael Wenderoth

## How to Use this Book

I want you to Get Real, Get Strategic, and Get Doing—so you can Get Promoted.

This book is laid out in a 3-step framework that helps you do exactly that, using the metaphors of the Rock, the Map, and the Snowball to illuminate the way.

I encourage you to bring your own challenges and goals at work and apply what you read to that situation. Reflect on the questions, do the exercises—that will make the concepts really sink in and will help you advance more rapidly.

The Rock (Chapters 3-7) represents hard truth ("Get Real"). We need to accept the hard truth and let go of dangerous myths. The Rock helps you make fundamental mindset shifts.

The Map (Chapters 9-11) shows how to be strategic ("Get Strategic"). We first need to see the forest from the trees. The Map helps you read the landscape to plan the most efficient and effective path.

The Snowball (Chapters 12-14) shows how to be tactical ("Get Doing"). We look at where to start and why, and how to put things together and get things to happen. The Snowball helps you take action because, without action, nothing happens.

We also look at how to tend and take care of The Snowball, so it becomes easier to grow and maintain—and does not get out of control.

What I am sharing with you works, so give it a chance.

## Foundations: 3 Pillars and How This Book Is Different

### The 3 "pillars" that I base my book upon

Many business and self-help books are based on the author's personal experience, or nowadays based on a few basic Google searches they conducted. More authors and speakers ought to let you know where or how they have drawn their conclusions, but few take the time to do so, or are even asked. I believe it matters. So, know that this book, and my coaching, is based on three important pillars:

1) **The evidence** - There is substantial research in the social sciences about what works and why it works. But most people don't study the evidence and rely instead on random advice and that is not just executives; many coaches are guilty of that too.

2) **My clients** - I have worked with thousands of diverse executives from around the globe, on the topics in this book. There is inherently some level of potential bias in drawing from this sample: People self-select into my coaching, I work with a specific socio-economic profile, etc. But the exposure to real situations and deep work allows me to see patterns—what works, common pitfalls—and be able to draw lessons from that.

One of my personal habits, which I once thought of as a curse, is that I take diligent notes and I review and analyze that collected "data" at set intervals. Only recently have I realized this habit has given me incredibly rich, useful information. Then, when I have to speak or write, I am forced to synthesize and draw conclusions, which sharpens my thinking. I understand the limitations of my data, but it serves as a valuable second pillar.

3) **My experience** - Before becoming an executive coach, I led a successful twenty-year career in senior roles in high growth companies across three continents. I am very careful not to project my experience on others because each client's situation is unique. But I have walked in their shoes. I know the stress of juggling multiple balls, the crazy reality of matrixed organizations, balancing the right long-term investments with hitting your numbers next month and dealing with office politics (yes, I have stories you wouldn't even believe). I get it. I know the pressures executives face. Many coaches, ironically, have never held a full-time job in their life.

I want clients to understand the principles and strategies and build the habits so they can apply them, long after we work together, in new situations. Because clients are focused on the practical, I share in this book numerous examples of how other clients have applied these concepts. I ask tough questions for you to reflect on, and I provide tools and exercises for you to apply.

**How this book is different from others, on the topic of power**

There are many excellent books on power but none that walk you through, step by step, how to build power at work, in your own situation. (And sorry, Robert Greene's bestseller, *The 48 Laws of Power*, is neither). My book is an attempt to fill this void. It reflects my focus as an executive coach: My clients come with real challenges, and they want to address them now. They don't usually have the time or inclination to read academic papers, or get feel-good advice, or have nonstop Socratic conversations. I need to help them responsibly because a lot is on the line.

So, this book is my attempt to create a guide, a playbook, which draws from and informs the largely successful executive coaching practice I have built. Many people will have you believe that you can't break down complex processes into an algorithm or decision tree. But throughout my career, I have always been obsessed with creating "playbooks"and over and over successfully have done that, ranging from construction processes to how doctors should straighten teeth with invisible braces to executing sales calls to how to lead a productive innovation process.

Enough with the preamble. Let's get started.

# CHAPTER 1

# Can You Handle the Truth?

*"The truth will set you free, but first it will piss you off!"*
*- Gloria Steinem*

You feel like you've done what you need to advance in your career… to get big things done in your current role that make you stand out… to get the edge that takes you upward… to be a change agent in your organization.

You've played by the rules as you understand them. But it's just… not… happening. You feel stuck or stalled, and you don't know why. Or you are moving into territory where it feels like you need to do something different to survive and thrive—but you are not sure exactly what that is.

Here are some harsh truths about being an executive in today's corporate environment:

- Being smart and an expert in your role is not enough.
- Hard work and productivity are not enough.
- Hitting—or even exceeding—your targets is not enough.

- Consistently good performance is not enough.
- Being loved by your team is not enough.

You strive to be authentic and have adopted the servant leadership mentality, and you're careful not to brag about your accomplishments or cozy up to upper-level management because of the negative image that sends.

You just know that being a team player, keeping your head down, and letting your actions and great work speak for itself will gain the notice of your bosses, and their bosses, and lead to your next promotion… and the one after that…

In other words, you believe in a "Just World."[2] Or worse, you follow what I call the "Kumbaya" school of leadership. You really believe that the workplace is a meritocracy… that your hard work stands on its own and will be recognized… that playing "office politics" is so obvious, unfair, unsavory, beneath you, and just not how things are done anymore… Instead, you gravitate to warm and inspiring Ted Talks about being authentic, positive, transparent, vulnerable as the answer.

Unfortunately, if that's your sole perspective, you're in for a rocky road. You'll find it very difficult to rise through the ranks—or get big and bold things done.

## Can You Handle the Truth?

Perhaps you've already recognized this at some level because you're stalled at your current position or your great initiatives aren't gaining traction... You're feeling demotivated, or worse, feeling like your career isn't progressing.

At the same time, you've seen colleagues promoted above you. And you've started to see some common threads in their paths, in how they spend their time, interact with key stakeholders, and "show up" in key situations. They may have even taken credit for the work of others. You are upset because you feel they are less qualified—that they are not as talented, smart, hardworking, or get the great results that you do.

Yet somehow, they not only keep their job, they thrive in the organization or seem to land well wherever they go. You're not sure exactly how they do what they do, but they do seem to be associated with success, rapidly on the rise, and in favor with those who run the company, despite their failings.

## The Big Lie and the (Not So) Secret Reality

You grew up and were told that hard work, putting in the hours, delivering on your goals, and being authentic are the keys to corporate success, leadership, and getting things done. After all, we are bombarded with this message.

But the hard truth is that it takes much more than strong performance to get ahead and get things done in organizations.

To *really* survive and thrive, you need to develop political skills—skills that help you understand power dynamics and help you build power. Leadership, after all, is about working with other people to get things done. It is about acts you take, based on the situation, to influence subordinates, peers, your bosses to achieve your goals. You have to manage competing interests, scarce resources and often a desire in others to maintain the status quo.

Organizations, even the ones who claim to be flat, transparent meritocracies—are anything but. Most seasoned executives grudgingly acknowledge this fact—but many still want to believe most organizations are fair places. And many young, aspiring leaders, in their first jobs, often refuse to believe "bad" things can happen to them.

The feel-good message about what it takes is reinforced by popular culture, MBA programs, and leadership training courses. It's what we read in superstar CEO biographies or fawning business magazine profiles, or hear in TED Talks, where the speakers paint a peaceful and rosy picture of how they made it to the top through grit, smarts and hard work. Getting likes and selling courses and books, after all, is important to them: The "leadership industry" is a big money-making machine.

History is written by the victors, as they say, so it's no wonder that the stories that leaders tell reinforce a narrative that casts them in a positive light while the real way they rose is usually scrubbed from the story.

We feel good hearing these stories as they confirm what we deeply want to believe.

*"All progress starts by telling the truth." – Dan Sullivan*

But we don't benefit from rosy, fictitious stories of how the world, organizations, and our peers at work supposedly operate. What we really benefit from is the hard truth, how organizations *really* operate even if that means seeing behind the curtain at how the sausage is actually made.

Navigating that hard reality is what this book, and my coaching, is about.

Many in the leadership industry, coaching field, and business schools are well-meaning but misguided. They train you on how the world and organizations *ought to work*. Name your favorite leadership trend: Be positive, be transparent, be vulnerable, be authentic, be a servant. I am sure your organization has these pinned to the wall or repeated them in training.

These are not bad things. But taken hook, line, and sinker, applied without realizing how organizations really function, you end up like Matt. In the spirit of transparency and "radical candor," Matt critiqued a senior leader, which was met with backlash. In the name of being vulnerable, Matt opened up about his shortcomings, which a peer exploited.

Those might seem like "rookie" mistakes, but even Matt made them! Why hadn't he been warned about this in his MBA program and "leadership training"? Why hadn't they given him basic street smarts? By glossing over and not exposing the hidden but real forces by which people make decisions, follow others, advance their agendas, we are setting up promising talent for failure. Good people get taken advantage of, instead of being fully prepared for the often brutal "real world".

It's like sending a lamb into a pack of wolves, or shielding your kids from bullies and bias, instead of sitting them down and giving them the hard truth and giving them the tools to recognize and manage what is likely to happen, and to ensure they not only don't get hurt, but they can prevail in the face of that reality.

## It's About Power

At the same time, there are those who would like you to believe these hidden forces are mysterious, complex, and can't be learned. People and organizations are indeed irrational, but they are irrational in very predictable ways.

And if you understand one fact of organizational life—power—it will help you advance, in very dramatic ways.

But you need to make several shifts in your thinking and how you spend your time, which we will walk you through in this book.

Power is misunderstood, underexamined, and underutilized by people like Matt.

The simple definition of power is being able to get your way in the face of opposition:

- *Power is relative* - You have more power than someone else if you are not dependent on them. Had Matt had more power, he would have seen warning signs and taken the right steps not to be ousted. Had Matt had more power, one of his great initiatives would have seen the light of day.
- *Power is everywhere* - It defines and exists in all social relationships.
- *Power is nothing more than a force* - A force that can be helpful if you are trying to make something happen in a complex environment, with competing interests.

What helps you diagnose power dynamics and build power, which in turn gets you promoted and amplifies your ability to get things done?

It all comes down to understanding who controls or possesses resources that are valued by others and then acting on that knowledge.

The key sources that build power:

1. Political and interpersonal skills (the ability to influence)
2. Your network and relationships (who you know)
3. Visibility and brand (who knows you)
4. Executive presence and communication skills (how you show up and are perceived)
5. Control of hard resources (strong tools at your disposal)

In Part I (the Rock), I'll walk you through the evidence that backs these up. In Part II (the Map) and Part III (the Snowball), we'll go through the steps to apply them to your situation...

It also helps to accept that not everyone has purity of intent and plays nice and fair.

The harsh truth is that the world is an *unjust* place: People of certain backgrounds are favored, bias sometimes prevails... the playing field is not level... and it never will be.

The sooner we accept these hard truths, the better. Because then we can be pragmatic, strategic, and deliberate in how we assess what we must do to reach our goals. Then we can actually focus on how to move the needle at work, and in our careers—and not just daydream about it.

That doesn't mean you can't still have fun at work and have humility and compassion—it just means you have to be attentive to the situation, particularly to the power structure.

That is ultimately what I want you to have and what I lay out for you in this book: a real guide on how to level up and focus on things you can change while at the same time not fretting about what cannot be changed, nor applying techniques that may feel good but ultimately are divorced from reality.

*The farther that you advance, the more that new skills become even more critical.*

## So Does Performance Matter?

Don't get me wrong: Your smarts, performance and working hard does help you (even if there is still plenty of evidence that people can go shockingly far without either).

It's just that performance is *not enough*. The farther you advance, the more that new skills become even more critical—leading through others, overcoming entrenched and competing interests, to name a few. Maybe being too authentic is holding you back. If you don't make this mindset shift, if you hold an overly rigid definition of who you are and what skills are important (which Matt was guilty of), you're in for a tough time.

### Be careful of "authenticity"

We live in a period of nonstop "authenticity." Bring your authentic self to work, become an authentic leader. The word has been so overused, it is in danger of losing all meaning. Moreover, there are strong arguments, to paraphrase an article in *Leadership Quarterly,* that "authentic leadership" theory is full of fundamental flaws, shaky reasoning, unsupported claims and is out of date with real corporate life.[3]

Do we need to be authentic, or be our true selves, to be effective in organizations?

While being authentic is certainly less taxing than behaving in ways that don't feel natural, there are plenty of situations where we might *not* want to be authentic. For example:

- Don't like the boss's plan? Criticizing it in public in ways that make the boss look bad, might be career limiting...
- Not entirely sure what caused the problem? Saying you have no idea and have no plan is not going to engender trust from your board, your customers, or your employees...
- Dislike a small point in a peer's proposal? Nit-picking every detail may just be plain aggravating to a person you need to work with...
- Presenting to non-technical leaders? Elaborating too much on every detail, you might lose valuable support....

There are plenty of instances where *not being authentic* (or what you perceive to be your authentic self) is the best course. For example:

- Being a little "fake" with a compliment or not digging at someone on a point that doesn't matter might ensure you have a better working relationship.
- Acknowledging an issue but showing up with confidence that it will get resolved—even if deep down you are not 100% certain—might be precisely what the situation calls for.
- Telling a story, rather than rattling off endless technical facts that may not be remembered, might connect better and sway your audience.

As Herminia Ibarra of London Business School so aptly lays out in the *Authenticity Paradox*, sometimes authenticity can be a crutch for sticking with things that are comfortable—when there's plenty of evidence that being uncomfortable is critical to learning new behaviors, behaviors that may help us grow and serve us in new situations.[4]

Do you have too rigid a sense of authenticity and yourself? Is there room for you to redefine and re-examine what it means to be authentic?

Is being "authentic" holding you back?

## Want to Be a Leader? Start Acting Like One

If you're not getting ahead, or you're feeling stalled, it's time to consider if what you have been doing up to this point is serving you well. As one "stalled" executive I worked with put it:

> *"I knew that the things that I did that got me here wouldn't get me to the next level, but I wasn't quite sure what those things I need to do at this new level are. I have a sense, but I don't really know. And the stakes are higher, the time window is shorter, and I don't want to mess around."*

Building and wielding power doesn't mean you have to be unethical or Machiavellian, if that is your worry (an aspect we will address later).

Understand power dynamics and build power, and you can:

- Avoid having your career halted or even derailed
- Enjoy promotions and financial rewards
- Gain more control over your career and future
- See your initiatives enjoy more impact
- Be able to overcome resistance to change—people and organizations are hardwired to favor the status quo

That's what my clients want and what I want success to look like for you.

**Success?**

If you're a person who thinks deeply—which I know you are if you picked up this book—your immediate question is probably, "What is the definition of success?"

My assumption in this book is that success is your ability to be more in charge of your life and be more fulfilled. That could mean you have more control and enjoyment over what you do, experience professional and personal growth, and get the recognition you want or deserve. Ideally, this is met with material rewards and perks, and more fulfilling opportunities—whether it's in your organization or elsewhere.

But to be clear: Only you define success.

If the above is not your definition of success, write down what you want. What does fulfillment look like to you? What do you want to optimize in your life?

Most of my clients want to get to the C-suite, make serious money, get big initiatives accomplished, set the course of their organization, or impact their industry.

But some of my clients are not trying to become the CEO. They want more fulfilling work, job security, a good nest egg, recognition, work-life balance, less frustration and stress, or have companies frequently reach out to them with compelling opportunities.

Success is personal and can shift at different points in your life.

So, think deeply about what you want: how you define success and your personal and professional goals. That will help you see how power can help you and which strategies will best serve you in that pursuit.

To level up, or advance, we often have to shed some habits, and learn powerful new ones. Athletes do it. Top performers do it. And you can, too.

If you don't take action now, what's at stake?

- Your job, advancement, and your satisfaction with your career and life

- Your ability to move ahead in a crucial period and keep growing
- The impact of your work

You don't want to be looking back years from now, wishing you had done things differently.

If you don't embrace the concepts I highlight in this book, chances are your savvier peers will and are probably doing so right now—and they will use power to their advantage, even advance right past you. In fact, mastering these concepts will help you make sense of what is happening around you and that knowledge just might save you.

**This book is NOT for you, if:**

- You are perfectly happy with where you are professionally and personally.
- You have no ambition or desire to learn the skills and strategies that are shown to propel you, and which you will increasingly need the longer you stay in and the higher you rise in your organization.
- You don't like to get the direct, unadulterated, uncomfortable truth—even if it is backed by evidence (you prefer to hear and read things that make you feel good or confirm your worldview).
- You believe in destiny and letting fate take its course.

If you are ready to shape your future, let's dive in. When you go through this transformation, you'll probably realize that you've been holding yourself back. You'll wonder why you didn't explore these concepts much earlier in your career.

### Not just for "Big Corporates"

The principles and strategies in this book work in companies big and small, and in business, non-profits, and government.

Wherever you have an organization of two or more people, power dynamics are at work that you must consider. Even entrepreneurs, who have a board, investors, or need to bring customers and employers to their side, gain huge benefits from understanding and building power.

When you develop and master these skills, you'll not only excel in your current position but will be able to apply them to new opportunities and excel from day one. The world is constantly changing, so it's critical to understand principles and have widely applicable frameworks. The context and tools may change, but the fundamentals don't.

I've coached executives of every stripe: representing wide-ranging industries, across cultures, and from every continent. I've coached ambitious university grads to seasoned executives about to retire. Trust me: The principles are universal; the strategies are widely applicable, even if the execution (tactics) may differ slightly based on each person's situation. The world, organizations, and people are much more alike than they are unalike.

# CHAPTER 2

# Three Reasons You Need This Book

When people approach me about coaching, it's generally because they are faced with one of three situations:

1. **They have stalled in their career.** They are not advancing at the pace they expected, and they are looking for the reasons why and solutions.

2. **They've just entered a new, higher stakes phase or situation,** a promotion, new job or role, for example, or working with a new boss or set of executives after a merger.

3. **Their career has not just stalled but totally been derailed,** and it seems like they have no future in the company, nor good prospects.

## 1. If You're Stalled...

You're smart and work hard, but you've seen one or more of the following things happen:

- You've missed a couple of cycles of promotions.
- Your initiatives and ideas don't get traction, or others have claimed them for their own.
- People you would not have expected are moving up (and past you). Even worse is knowing that you're smarter than those people. You're better at your job. You're more qualified. Yet they are promoted above you.
- You don't get the high-profile assignments and instead are given projects nobody wants or the ones you are already good at.
- The top people aren't coming to you seeking advice or asking you to take on initiatives. It's like you're invisible.

The good news is that you still have time to recover and take action.

You've probably seen colleagues and others who seem to have a different skill set and have been able to leverage it for further advancement. But you don't feel confident, or comfortable, in your ability to do the same.

## 2. If You're in a New High Stakes Situation…

You might be transitioning to a new role, like a promotion to VP, or hired at a new company, where it's critical to make an impact and impression in the first 90 days.

Or there is an upcoming corporate takeover, the ground is suddenly shifting under your feet, and you want to be ahead of the change and land solidly under new management.

You know you need to bring your "A" game. You must prove yourself quickly. But you have no idea how to deal with other high-level executives.

This is an intimidating situation (but also one filled with opportunity if you handle it well).

In this scenario:

- The expectations of you are now much higher—as are the rewards.
- The spotlight is now on you in a way it wasn't before.
- You know you're dealing with savvier executives.
- If you are doing things that represent change, which involves new ways of doing things, you can be assured you will get resistance.

Say your company gets taken over by a big multinational. Not only do you have a new boss, but they're only going to take one division head of the two that have been combined. Of course, you want it to be you.

Or perhaps a mentor guided you into a new, higher position or to head a high-profile project in your organization. They've vouched for you. You don't want to let them down.

In either case, you're facing a lot of pressure. All eyes are on you. That's where it's really important to step up. If you perform and manage the situation skillfully, you'll not only keep the job, but you'll be in the running for future advancement... maybe even be put on the fast-track.

You don't want to spin your wheels or lose precious time that you don't have. Worse, sometimes there aren't many people you can turn to for sound advice. Those below you don't have the knowledge, those around you might not be ones you can open up to fully about your struggle, and with those above you, you are afraid of looking weak.

## 3. If Your Career Has Derailed...

Despite being very accomplished:

- You've been fired or "sent out into right field" (sidelined or benched) into a downgraded position.
- You've lost a power struggle and been demoralized.

In these situations, even if you have not been fired, it's doubtful that you can turn things around at your organization. More likely, you must now rebuild your career elsewhere.

In these cases, it's important to let go of anger and bitterness. You must recognize that your approach must change. This time you have to do things right.

### The cream does not rise to the top

When Jill (not her real name) came to me, she was stunned. She had an MBA from a top-tier school, spoke multiple languages, and was a consistent top 10% performer. She was driven, intelligent, and personable. She had handwritten thank-you notes from the CEO posted on her wall.

As she put it: "I was universally liked across the company, a team player who put in more hours than anyone else," she said. "I was heads down on delivering results, shared my inner self and built trust... everything I was trained and even coached to do."

She trusted that her efforts would be recognized, and that the cream would naturally rise to the top.

Yet this rising young executive found herself strategically ousted from her position in an internal power play... instead of on the fast-track to a corner office that she expected.

Her mistake? Instead of only putting in long hours at her desk delivering great work, she should have been making herself visible in her organization, networking with top executives, and making sure that great work she was doing was noticed by the right people. She should have also watched her back and not assumed everyone had purity of intent. That's part of being realistic and pragmatic.

After this setback, Jill learned her lesson. Three years later, she recognizes reality and not only does good work but also plays the game. She is thriving at her current company and rising quickly. She even advises young people starting their careers that doing well in your job is only part of the success equation.[5]

## Looking for Solutions in the Wrong Places

Whatever the scenario, whether you're stalled, faced with a high-stakes situation, or derailed, the underlying issue is the same: What got you *here*, won't get you *there*.

*Your behaviors and interactions got you this far...*
*but are no longer enough.*

In other words, your skills got you this far... but are no longer enough to get you to the next level.

There is a fundamental shift in how you must show up and operate. It's more complex. It can make your head spin, and it's daunting to determine where to focus and best spend your time. You don't want to lurch and grab any idea or advice you hear, but that's what so many people do.

If you're reading this book, you might already realize this at a subconscious level. At this stage, you understand that performance alone is not enough. And that going it alone, with your present skills, has its risks.

When you understand a single force—power—you begin to see the organization with new, intelligent eyes. So, my goal is to unpack power for you. It's a word that has many negative associations, leading us to shy away from it. But it is omnipresent, and we ignore it at our peril. As Michel Foucault said, "Power is everywhere."[6]

Why do some people have more power than others?

It's actually quite simple: You have more power than someone else if you control resources that they value—resources they can't get elsewhere. Think of a negotiation—if you have something unique that the other party values highly, you are likely to get what you want from them in exchange. If you can get what they offer from three other people, they have less power. That means you have leverage, or more power, in relation to them. Having unique and valued resources makes a company or product valuable and powerful, just like it makes people more powerful.

We mainly think of power as control over budget and decisions—allowing you to reward and punish.

But power can come from a wide variety of sources:

- Titles or positions
- Expertise or knowledge
- Access or information
- Credibility or reputation
- Relationships or networks
- Interpersonal and political skills
- Personal qualities
- and more...

If you understand what can increase or decrease your unique value in the eyes of others, you can build power (gain leverage), making it easier—if you so choose—to exercise that power to get what you want.

Hold this thought. This simple observation can take you extremely far, and it holds the key as we start our journey by embracing the Rock.

**Is power a dirty word?**

Power is the ability to get your way in the face of opposition.

The problem is in the connotation it brings. Most people view power as synonymous with *coercion*—you have the power to make someone do something... to force your will. Sounds evil.

In truth, power is merely a tool. It's neither bad nor good. It exists in all social relationships.

But because power through history has been associated with dictators and corrupt leaders, we associate it with evil.

Yes, you can use power to make people's lives miserable—but you can also wield it for worthy goals that improve lives and organizations.

# PART I
## The Rock

"Better the hard truth, I say, than the comforting fantasy."

- Carl Sagan

# CHAPTER 3

# 5 Dangerous Myths That Derail Careers

Based on what you've read so far, you might be in denial, starting to get angry, or moving to grudging acceptance.

To recap points that upset people the most:

- Great performance is not enough to get you ahead.
- Trying to be "authentic" is probably holding you back.
- Building power is the key to helping you the most.

If you are like most people I work with, you need to start by taking a deep, honest look in the mirror.

To move forward, we need to first address five myths. When you reflect and admit how they are holding you back, you'll make the important mindset shifts that are critical to moving forward.

# Myth #1: The World Is Fair.

You still adhere to this myth if you say, "My great performance will get me ahead, get me seen, and get me promoted."

Remember how the "just world" myth gets perpetuated. Many of us are told from a young age that keeping your head down and doing good work will get you ahead. Think about the TED Talks, the leadership training programs you attended, the CEO biographies focusing on their hard work and inspirational ascent. Remember people are attracted to these stories because it is what we want to believe.

Ask yourself:

- How has the "just world" message been ingrained in me?
- How might this have served me—or hurt me?
- How might this impede me from learning new skills or behaviors?
- Looking around in my own organization at what is being promoted and rewarded: Who is rising? What path did they take? How do they spend their time? How do they show up? How does that compare to those who are not rising or have left?
- Take a frank look at what is *really* being rewarded, not at what leaders and HR say will get rewarded: What do I see?

To make meaningful progress, you must let go of believing the world is fair. You need skills adapted to how the world *actually operates—not on how you wish it would.*

# Myth #2: Power and Politics Are Evil.

You adhere to this myth if you say, "Power and politics are nasty, underhanded, and unsavory. It's beneath me and something I just can't bring myself to do."

Or if you say, "I won't self-promote or spend my time networking. That's not doing your job… In fact, it's compensating for not being able to do your job."

Or if you say, "I can't do politics or build power *and* stay authentic."

Why does this view prevail?

Write down words and the names of people that come to mind when you hear the word "power". Do the same for the word "politics". The associations are always negative. The first people that are named, when I ask executives for examples of people with strong power and political skills, are [name your dictator], [name your brash CEO].

But if you look at the textbook definition of power, it doesn't imply anything of the sort. What about leaders or executives on *Time Magazine's* List of Most Influential People?

Ask yourself:

- In the chart below, which words do I most associate with power and politics?
- How has power and politics, at work or in life, affected me?

- Some say power corrupts, but can powerlessness also corrupt?
- Is it more important to be right or for the right things to happen?
- What might I learn, and possibly even adopt, from powerful and political people that I don't like, but who get their way?
- With more power, what might I gain?
- What am I most worried about if I embrace power and politics?

Because we have negative associations of power and politics, we throw out the baby with the bath water. There is lots we can learn, even from people we don't like—and learning from them doesn't mean we have to become them.

The truth is that the same political savviness that propels toxic people to the top can also help propel humble people. And what might you gain—or are able to do that you currently cannot—if you get to the top or if you have more power?

# Reconceive Your Negative Associations of Power and Politics

| NEGATIVE | NEUTRAL OR POSITIVE |
|---|---|
| Bragging / Self-promoting | Ensuring your achievements are seen and you get credit |
| Currying favor / Brown-nosing | Building positive relationships. Making people feel good about themselves. Helping people with their agenda |
| Speaking up/ Hogging airtime | Making sure you are heard—and not invisible |
| Wasteful small talk | Breaking the ice, getting to know people, forming a bond |
| Manipulating people | Persuasion and influence |
| Being deceitful, misrepresenting facts, lying so people don't see things | Framing info so people do see things; strategically putting things in context; managing the narrative |
| "Acting" and being fake | Ensuring you have presence and are perceived well; attending to what the situation calls for |
| Cherry picking what work you do | Ensuring you are engaged in meaningful work |
| Being "bossy" and ordering people around | Being clear |
| Hogging the limelight | Ensuring you and others who deserve it are recognized |
| Being aggressive | Being assertive |
| Demanding | Asking for what you need—and making a strong case for it |

## Myth #3: The Rules Don't Apply to Me.

You buy into this myth if you say, "I'm different. The 'rules' for getting ahead don't apply to people who look like me [age/gender/ethnicity] or apply in my situation [organization/country/industry/company size]."

These views prevail because we like to focus on our differences and are attracted to shiny "new theories" about how the rules have changed.

While many groups have it harder, due to systemic bias (the world is definitely not fair), there is also substantial evidence that humans have much in common, and the principles by which we operate and relate to one another in organizations are remarkably unchanged. In an excellent review of why theories of power still apply across time and contexts, Jeff Pfeffer highlights fundamental—and unchanging—social and organizational dynamics:[7]

- We gravitate to and organize ourselves in hierarchies.
- There are universal drivers that lead to perceptions of competence.
- We favor those who are like us, make us feel good about ourselves, and help us advance our agendas.
- Deep down we all want to feel connected and work with "winners".

Ask yourself:

- What has led me to believe I am different, that my situation is different, and that the principles don't apply or won't work?
- Am I using "I'm different" as an excuse, or as information?
- How might I test these assumptions or beliefs?
- If I don't focus on ways to build power, where does that leave me?

Pfeffer, who has taught on power for decades at Stanford, has observed that understanding power and politics has *most benefited* women, minorities and people of color in his courses. They are more apt to report greater benefit from the course concepts than their white male peers, which was similar to a finding from a survey of 240 executives that I conducted in 2021 with Inbal Demri.[8]

In my private coaching practice (70% of my clients are women or minorities), I notice the exact same thing: These clients *really* benefit the most.

Precisely because people from these historically marginalized groups have traditionally had less power, the process of understanding how to build and harness power, through their own daily actions, arms them in powerful ways. Of course, acknowledging power is at play is one thing, but really understanding how it works is another—and being able, and willing, to harness it is quite another. This last point—helping people really use power—is where I have found 1-1 coaching really helps.

Given the playing field is clearly not level, that many well-intended diversity programs have been shown to fail and can do more harm than good,[9] and the "feel-good" Kumbaya leadership advice has not been helping you—it behooves you to really learn how power can be built at work and used in your everyday life.

## Myth #4: Others Are Wrong.

Have you ever thought to yourself... "I'm right; it's others in my organization who are wrong."

Or said: "They just don't see my greatness."

We tend to see the world through our own eyes, and as multiple research studies have shown, we all rank ourselves above average.[10] So, who's below average?

Ask yourself:

- Have multiple people given me similar feedback that I just won't accept?
- Could something that I'm doing have an unintended consequence?
- Could I be less judgmental about others I don't like or agree with? Might they be doing something right—something to learn from?
- If I keep hitting dead ends, is it time to consider a new approach?

Extracting lessons from others doesn't mean you will become them. You don't need to change yourself or your core values; you just need to be more open to trying out new behaviors and skills that can help you grow.

Maybe you're not so great. That might be a hard pill to swallow, but the sooner you accept that you might be wrong, the faster you can test and incorporate new skills.

### Self-awareness: 4 ways to get it

Numerous studies have shown that understanding yourself (self-awareness, self-knowledge) is one of the most critical elements to effective leadership. If you want to improve anything, you need to have an accurate assessment of how you stack up, your strengths and weaknesses—so you can target them.

How do you get an accurate read of yourself? Here are 4 areas to explore:

1) **Assessments:** There are many personality and leadership assessments that can provide useful insights. But be careful: They have limitations, and many have no scientific basis (the Myers Briggs, to cite one well-known example). That doesn't invalidate their use, but companies often make dangerous conclusions about people based on them. The assessment industry is a huge business, so the survey your company swears by may be more a result of marketing and popularity than anything real and substantive.

2) **Feedback:** Your boss, peers, reports, mentors can provide feedback through written reviews or discussion. You'll want to establish a trusting relationship, so you're not being fed what you want to hear, or what they want you to hear.

3) **An external coach:** Coaches can provide a needed outside view, be a sounding board and safe space to share things you wouldn't want colleagues to know. But coaches also may not fully see into your situation. There's also no established training of coaches, so make sure to understand their background and approach.

4) **Journaling and self-reflection:** Studies have shown the positive impact of observation and thoughtful reflection. Build in the practice of reflecting on your day and taking someone else's perspective—these are simple, cathartic, and effective. To improve your communications, watch a video replay of yourself presenting. It's painful, but I guarantee you'll immediately pick up one thing you can do better.

## Myth #5: These Skills Cannot Be Learned.

If you believe political skills and building power are innate skills ("only extroverts can network"), you have a fixed mindset and won't get far.

Ask yourself:

- What new skills have I learned in the past?
- How did I improve them over time, especially if parts were difficult to adopt?
- How did those new skills benefit me?
- Am I in a "what got me here, won't get me there" moment?
- Am I staying in the same role at work because I do the same thing over and over and it's comfortable and valuable to others (a "competency trap")?
- What effective techniques have I dismissed because of negative associations?

There are certainly some things that are hard or impossible to change, like our skin color, gender, height, maybe even aspects of our personalities.

But there is plenty that we can change. Research by Carol Dweck at Stanford and Angela Duckworth at the University of Pennsylvania shows that those with a "growth mindset" and "grit"—those who see problems as opportunities, who are willing and believe they can put in the energy and learn what is needed to advance, tend to fare much better than those with a "fixed mindset," who believe they are born with set skills.[11]

The takeaway: Have a more flexible definition of yourself and what you are capable of. If you refocus on how something can be learned, you are likely to go further.

## Sam's shift

Sam (not her real name) was talented and smart but a bit shy, which led her to be heads down at work and not speak up in meetings. She wanted to get promoted in her consumer goods company but kept getting passed over. One peer actually took Sam's insights and launched a much heralded, breakthrough new product.

After Sam and I started working together, she observed that being quiet was having unintended consequences: Top executives only saw her as a one-dimensional contributor and her boss saw her as being content where she was, even afraid to take charge.

Sam got out of her own way. She realized her heads down hard work focus, partly coming from her Asian upbringing, had gotten her hired but was now holding her back (Myth #1). Moreover, solely being smart was not what was most valued at the director level and above in her company. The fast risers included people like that peer, who took Sam's insights to launch the new product and got promoted. Was that stealing Sam's idea, or had Sam falsely assumed the idea would make her shine, and not done enough to roll out the idea across the company (Myth #2)?

"I can't possibly be like some of my aggressive, outspoken, highly connected—and kind of stupid—

peers. Also, this is a young, flat, tech-like company, and we always say the best ideas win," she said (Myth #3). Nevertheless, she re-examined some of her assumptions about others (Myth #4), and the rigid assumption that she had to be loud and aggressive just to be "heard", that she needed to kiss the butts of her boss and others in order for them to know her goals.

She built power by being more assertive: She made her ambitions known, built relationships with top people, and communicated more clearly (Myth #5). She spoke with her boss 1-1 about her career goals, sought advice from a senior executive that turned into sponsorship, and started to make specific recommendations in team meetings.

Three months later, she was promoted. Her senior leaders told her that had she not spoken to them, had she not started to lead and propose ideas, that they would have looked outside to fill the position.

Sam confronted the five myths, which shifted her mindset. This got her taking seemingly small actions. Those actions were strategic, however, and they made a huge difference for Sam—and they can for you too.

## Stop Doing the Things That Made Me Successful?

To be clear, I am not saying to stop doing good work, or to start doing shitty work (although look how many people have consistently weak performance and still get promoted—I hope that helps you accept the truth and bothers you enough to take action).

The sooner you confront these five myths and shift your mindset, the better off you will be. It's most likely to result in a critical shift in how you spend your time.

Think about when you first learned a new skill or retooled your technique, like with a sport you play. It was foreign. It took time, effort, maybe required you to observe others who were good at it. Maybe you even had to unlearn certain habits. Perhaps it was initially uncomfortable. Making that change shifted your game, it took you to the next level.

But being uncomfortable is not the main point. The main point is to ask yourself: "Under what logic is what I am doing today shown to work?" That's the critical question because the logic of what you are doing today may very well be built on myths. Challenge your existing perspectives, open your mind to new possibilities—and realize you have choices. And making some of those choices will set you free and propel you.

Myths, of course, run deep and can be incredibly hard to dislodge, so let's take the next step, which is to examine overwhelming evidence that drills down into what does lead to career success—to getting promoted, becoming more effective, amplifying your impact. Then you can concentrate on how you level up in these critical areas and start to move the needle.

### What's good for you vs what's good for the organization

You've seen it repeatedly. A leader drives their organization into the ground, or gets poor results, but still walks off with huge bonuses, a golden parachute, or plenty of job offers. Or the inverse: Employee sacrifices and does what is best for the organization but does not personally benefit, or maybe gets passed over.

There are plenty of situations where what is good for the individual is not good for the organization, and vice versa. Alignment of interests is the ultimate goal, but it's important to keep this fact of organizational life in mind.

Given organizations have become so messed up, make sure you take care of yourself! Seek a win for your team and a win for the organization. But be wary—or at least not be naïve in organizational life. Sadly, not everyone has your best interests at heart, and quite often those that do the actual work are not rewarded for it.

# CHAPTER 4

# Leaving Fantasy Land

If hard work and the Kumbaya school of leadership (transparency, vulnerability, authenticity) don't make you a rising star in your organization… what does?

The key is understanding power dynamics and building power. And power comes from five sources:

1. Political Skills
2. Strong Networks
3. Visibility and Brand
4. Executive Presence and Communication Skills
5. Control of Hard Resources

Let's take one quick example that illustrates these in action.

John (not his real name) was a senior product manager hoping to rise in his mid-sized industrial firm. He had a decent relationship with his boss and was well respected. By all accounts John did a good job and over time would probably rise through normal (slow) seniority.

John was ambitious. Wanting more and knowing the four other product managers—his peers but also his competitors—wanted the same thing, he got proactive.

Spotting an emerging opportunity in a new geography, John raised his hand to lead a cross-functional initiative to get that region on board. He got initial support from his boss and then approached a senior director with a plan.

When he became the head of the project, John called meetings, set the agenda, enlisted diverse parts of the company to help, and provided updates to upper management. He even secured resources to bring in a consultant.

More importantly, he met regularly with his boss, the senior director, a regional VP—and had a monthly 1-to-1 with the CEO, who took interest in the growth opportunity. In those meetings, John was able to build a more personal relationship, showcase his knowledge, and become the "go to" person. Others around the company took notice that John had the ears and confidence of upper management.

Before long, John stood out among his peers, and even before the next promotion cycle, he had an offer to lead the product group or take on a senior role to lead the region.

John was proactive, and exemplifies the five areas that propel us:

1. **Political skills:** He was attuned to the agenda of the company and the key people who could move his career forward. As a result, he proposed a strategic

project with the blessing of his boss, and then carefully cultivated relationships with those who were critical to its success, and his success.

2. **Strong Network:** By taking a cross-functional role, he positioned himself at the center of the action. He had access to diverse experts across the company, enabling him to broker information and build the new region's business, in ways that mattered to key decision makers.

3. **Visibility and Brand:** Because he ran meetings, sent updates, reported out to the CEO and VP, he stood out and became known while other product managers were not. That gave him an opportunity to share his background and cultivate his brand as a rising leader. The project was featured in the company quarterly newsletter, the consulting firm highlighted his work in an industry magazine, and the CEO invited him to present at the company All-Hands.

4. **Executive Presence and Communication Skills:** John had a technical background. Knowing he would have to present to the C-Suite, he asked his boss to sponsor him for a public speaking course—and he wisely sought out a senior executive and his boss to coach and advise him before every big presentation. He paid more attention to how he dressed and showed up, observing how the leadership meetings committees ran. The regional VP got invested in John's success and provided pointers but also started

to compliment John in closed C-Suite discussions about succession planning.

5. **Control of Hard Resources:** John was able to secure money to hire a consultant and within months secured a launch budget and two junior high potentials to report to him for the project duration. He was adept at influencing and bringing key department heads to the project, but it helped to have resources he could deploy quickly.

Check. Check. Check. Check. Check.

John was ambitious and proactive. He took strategic and deliberate steps to grow his career. He was also savvy and avoided outshining his boss, making sure to thank his boss and others publicly. He worried less about his product management peers and found ways for them to help the project which gave them exposure. He also had to deal with some unruly department heads, but his strong allies and sponsors helped him manage them.

Did John's rise require bare knuckled power moves and underhanded maneuvering?

No.

Was it difficult?

No, but it took effort.

Surprisingly, most people don't take strategic and bold steps like John did, hoping instead they will be "identified" and handed opportunities. Others mistakenly think power will come to them only after they get promoted. But as we saw with John, power can be built at any time.

And, if you think John is somehow a productivity beast for taking on all the added work, resources and other people started to come his way as he built power as the leader of the project.

His life got easier, not harder.

Was John flawless? No. He flubbed his first presentation but quickly got feedback and asked for the training. Was he liked by all his peers? No. Was his work stellar? Parts were, but he was also about to manage perception and how it was presented. A funny thing happened when it became clear John's stock was rising: More people wanted to be associated with him. That's what happens when you build power.

Was there some element of luck in John's case? Sure, but as they say, "The more I practice (the right things), the luckier I get". (Keep in mind, at the same time, another cross functional initiative arose to manage a back-end process. John considered that opportunity but determined it would not nearly have had as much impact on the company or his career).

Some people do what John did but then *fail to capitalize* on how much power they have built—and how they can then use that to further amplify their work, or to ask for that promotion ahead of cycle. John had no qualms, in the right moments, to ask for what he needed, be that resources and later a promotion reporting to the CEO, which also took him out from the shadow of his boss.

John engineered his success and built power to help him do it.

Understanding what could propel his rise, what would build his power, and getting coaching along the way really opened his eyes—and accelerated his ascent.

### Don't become a doormat: create value, *but also claim it*

Many of my clients are true team players. But many get taken advantage of—they get upset that a peer or boss stole their ideas, took credit for their work in private, even sabotaged their success.

Do "takers" always win the day? Can you be a "giver" and still succeed?

For "givers", there's good and bad news and a silver lining. The good news, shared by Adam Grant in *Give and Take*, is that givers can be amazingly successful—and do better than takers.

But the bad news is that givers also do extremely poorly. (Imagine a bell curve, with success on the x axis: Givers occupy the two far ends of that curve). They do poorly because they get taken advantage of. They become doormats.

The silver lining—and the important lesson—is that givers can end up on the better end of the bell curve, but they need to protect themselves and advocate for themselves. They should not always assume everyone plays nice and fair. Accepting the reality of organizational life and building personal power is a huge part of that. Value creators can also be value claimers![12]

Take John, the product manager. By being proactive and bringing the new region online, he created value. The company benefited, many stakeholders benefited, employees in that new group benefited.

John enjoyed personal growth, exposure, and new knowledge. But let's be honest—he also wanted professional growth: recognition, new opportunities given to rising stars, a promotion and a better salary and bonus.

A savvy peer could have swooped in, taken credit for John's work, or jumped in to lead the region— effectively claiming (or stealing) the value that John created. To ensure that did not happen, John built strong alliances with key stakeholders who would support him, made sure people he worried about reciprocated before he trusted them completely— and when it came time, made his strong case and asked for the promotion. He didn't assume good things would just happen. By doing so, John ended up on the right side of the bell curve.

## Learning From Those We May Not Like

People who use the strategies we saw in John's case are the ones who get promoted. They understand how important the five sources of power are to success.

But many of those who ascend are even bolder, more aggressive, not our cup of tea—and often not even half as "technically competent" or smart as John.

They repulse us but "succeed"—which is exactly why we should study them closely. First, studying them tells you what the organization really values or promotes. Second, if they can ascend or get things done on such weak performance, imagine what you could do with both great performance and their great skills?

If you can understand the *principles* they use, how they tap into the five sources of power, you can then think creatively, like John, on how to apply and adapt those same sources to your own situation, to help yourself, or to meet your goals.

*"When you are furious, first be curious."*

Focus on what you can learn from these people because clearly some of the things they are doing are working.

As you observe your more ascendant and "successful" peers and colleagues to see how they deploy these strategies for their own advancement, or to get things done, you should also compare them to those who seem to be getting nowhere.

Be clinical about it. Look at what people in both groups actually do, not what you hear or are told (people bend the truth all the time).

We'll do this exercise more fully in Part II, but here's what some of my clients found, and I am sure you will too:

A star colleague is never at his desk. He's always in meetings with people and seems to have good rapport or is always bantering about something they seem to care about personally, like a sports team, their alma mater, or their shared background at a previous company.

He's always having lunch with people—critical people, or people with specific and useful information. He doesn't show up to some routine meetings and, in fact, blows them off. Yet he seems to always be called in to key meetings, or his name appears on email chains. Sometimes he just shows up, and though he doesn't know anything about the topic at hand, talks with authority about it… so much so that people want to schedule time with him afterwards.

And he's on a pet project favored by the CEO.

Check. Check. Check.

It's many of those same elements at play:

- Political skills
- Strong Networks
- Visibility and Brand
- Executive Presence and Communication Skills

- Control of Hard Resources

These sources can build power and propel you in ways that performance by itself simply can't. In fact, coupled with performance, they can supercharge you. That's why it's never been more important to understand these concepts for navigating the corporate environment and building your power in an organization.

Not only will it help you thrive in your current company, but it will help you hit the ground running when opportunities at other companies pop up and you switch jobs.

These days, spending your entire career with one business is rare. Once you have mastered this playbook, you're well-equipped for anywhere you go, even if you decide to reinvent yourself.

**1-minute tip: ww_d?**

**How to (literally) get out of your own way**

The biggest barrier people have to building power and navigating office politics is themselves.

Maybe because of your upbringing, what you were told, or the fact that people who succeed or have power seem to do things you feel are unfair, or you don't like: They self-promote, they take credit, they sound bold.

But as we saw, you don't have to become those people—but you might just be able to learn from them.

And one of the most effective ways to get out of your own way is to get out of your own mind.

The next time you have a challenge or can't figure out what to do to build power, think of five people who have power. They can be politicians, CEOs, celebrities, that peer you detest but is so smooth in getting their way—or even maybe you a few years back when you were rising.

Now, ask yourself what would [Person #1] do in my situation. Write down in 30 seconds all the strategies they would apply or go about solving your problem.

Now what would person #2 do?

Now what would person #3 do?

And so on...

Chances are you generated an incredible list—and you probably got out of your own head.

My guess is that someone on that list, in a matter of less than a few minutes, might have a strategy you could apply. Or a strategy that could be tweaked to fit you and your situation? Or maybe the exercise quickly got you to think differently and may lead you somewhere useful. It got you unstuck, seeing possibility.

The exercise is: **What Would [so and so] Do**?

By allowing yourself to literally get out of your own head and think like someone else, you can escape the tracks in our thinking—the mindset that restricts us.[13]

Are you starting to let go of your old way of thinking? Are you starting to see how those repulsive people are pretty competent and sharp on a different dimension?

One executive I worked with who went through this exercise was quite upset. She realized that the colleague she observed focused her time relentlessly. She relentlessly made her bosses look good and would even leave update meetings early if she wasn't on the agenda. That peer spoke with confidence, and she highlighted the complexity of her work while peers with more complex projects assumed the leadership committee would see right through that. When problems hit, she shifted their focus and usually got more resources to solve the issue.

Without hesitation, she asked for things, delegated work to her reports or peers or even other teams, highlighted her team's work—and spoke up about what she needed more of to get a job done.

My client was dismayed that nobody could see it, it was so obvious… and that nobody called this peer out for her behavior.

Quite the opposite, in fact. That peer was viewed as in command and always able to get things done (even if she wasn't the one who did it). She knew her way around the organization chart—and as a result was first in line for advancement. Why? Because she had visibility, managed her reputation, was associated with positive and important things inside the company, and was confident. She was perceived by those who matter to be authoritative, a leader, and powerful.

And because of that, another interesting thing happened:

Her visibility, or maybe the LinkedIn posts she made highlighting her team's achievements, attracted good things on the outside. Recruiters would approach her for compelling opportunities. She even confided to my client that her boss gave her a raise off-cycle, so she would stay when she mentioned an attractive offer she was entertaining.

All the principles worked together to build power. They worked for this more "political" executive my client detested— but also, if you recall carefully, for John, the product manager.

## Should I trust? Think twice and proceed with caution

Does power lead to trust dilemmas? And is that a problem since trust seems to be a strong force that can really make an organization function smoothly?

First, there is strong evidence that when people are in trusting environments, you get better performance results. We believe we can speak our mind, disagree, and believe others have our back. Surfacing problems – rather than burying them – brings out the collective wisdom and insight in the team.

Amy Edmondson has done compelling work on psychological safety, which has been shown to lead to better work environments and better performance.[14] Some of her research was done in hospitals. When nurses felt like they could correct doctors, fewer overall errors occurred.

However, creating such an environment is *not* easy. We should strive for these organizations but tread with caution, especially assuming the environment is in place. For example, criticizing a boss publicly can be a career limiting move. I have seen backlash and retaliation used against well-meaning and frankly naïve people.

With workplace trust at an all-time low, be careful about whom you trust. And all the more reason, if you rise to the top or have power to shape the culture, to use your power to set the right tone and environment.

Blindly trusting can be dangerous. Don't always believe the hype in your organization: the feel-good phrase to trust and be transparent may be on the wall and in the handbook, but look at what really happens:

Are people who speak out rewarded (or not punished)?

Who is getting promoted and did they embody those behaviors on their way up?

What is the person's track record, especially a boss who comes in from outside?

Be wary of what people say (they always say good things in public)—look more at their past and what they have done.

To protect yourself, temper your trust, as Rod Kramer, an expert on the topic, advises us so well.[15] Look into people's past track record. Take small steps and see if they are reciprocated. Be wary when you are invited in to speak your mind about a boss in a 360. Be careful in showing vulnerability because that too can backfire—making you look weak or indecisive.

So, yes, trust is the ideal. But approach with caution!

# CHAPTER 5

# What the Evidence Really Says

Thus far, I've asserted that what you believe works—authenticity, transparency, and vulnerability—doesn't match reality. In this chapter, I'll present the evidence that the concepts I've shared in this book so far, and that will appear in upcoming chapters, are real. This is the research I've based this book on and what I bring to executives I work with.

This is typically dry, academic material. It often doesn't see the light of day, which is a shame since it is well researched and can be used to help us. But it's important that you are exposed to more objective proof, the social science evidence. It will help you see what really drives success, and it will create confidence and trust in what will come in the rest of the book.

In this chapter and the next one, I summarize or share details from many studies. **If you are in a hurry, go straight to the "Takeaways" section highlighted at the end of each section.** If you want details of the research, you can review the resources section at the back of the book.

Later, we'll look at examples of how clients have applied each area, so you can see what we are talking about in action.

As you read, ask yourself:

- What are the implications of this hard evidence for you?
- How have these played out in your past life or organizations?
- And most importantly, what could you do differently to get unstuck or ahead?

You will then be prepared, with a solid departure point, as we leap from The Rock to The Map.

## The Evidence

Understanding power and building power will help you get promoted and get more done.

To return to our simple definition, power is the ability to get things done in the face of opposition. You have power to the extent you possess or control resources that others value. Power is relative.

What are the sources that increase our power, and how can we use that knowledge?

Power comes from two main sources: "hard" and "soft". Think of "hard" sources as the possession or control of tangible resources, like a budget or being able to veto a decision. This is sometimes called structural or positional power. Think of "soft" sources as coming from your ability to influence, such as building rapport or enlisting support from others.

"Hard" and "soft" sources can be used to persuade—or coerce—others. Power is nothing more than a force, and you can have power but choose not to exercise it.

You can visualize the sources of power on a simple 2 x 2 grid below.

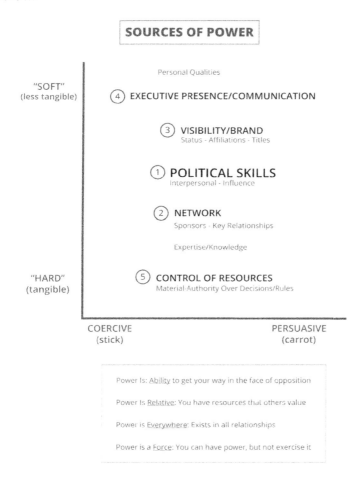

**SOURCES OF POWER**

"SOFT" (less tangible)

Personal Qualities

④ EXECUTIVE PRESENCE/COMMUNICATION

③ VISIBILITY/BRAND
Status · Affiliations · Titles

① POLITICAL SKILLS
Interpersonal · Influence

② NETWORK
Sponsors · Key Relationships

Expertise/Knowledge

"HARD" (tangible)

⑤ CONTROL OF RESOURCES
Material·Authority Over Decisions/Rules

COERCIVE (stick)          PERSUASIVE (carrot)

Power Is: Ability to get your way in the face of opposition

Power Is Relative: You have resources that others value

Power is Everywhere: Exists in all relationships

Power is a Force: You can have power, but not exercise it

A Google search will provide an overwhelming—and frankly not so helpful—list of the "sources of power." These include positions, titles, status, affiliation, expertise, information, networks, appearance, personal attributes to name a few.[16]

These are the five critical sources of power that you need to know:

1. Political Skills
2. Networks and Relationships
3. Visibility and Brand
4. Executive Presence and Communication Skills
5. Control of Hard Resources

I've singled out these five for two reasons. First, the evidence of their link to career success is overwhelming, as we shall see. Second, across my global coaching practice, they are consistently the top areas that most rapidly help executives I work with ascend.

Let's examine each source. Understand *why* they create power, and you will be way ahead in the game.

## 1. Political Skills

You probably have no shortage of examples or personal experiences where those who were more "political" or savvy had more success climbing the ladder, got bigger bonuses or pay raises, or even were able to get more things done.

It turns out the empirical research backs this finding.

Extensive research by Gerald Ferris and colleagues found that people with stronger political skills received higher performance evaluations and were rated as more effective leaders.[17] Ferris defines political skill as "the ability to effectively understand others at work, and to use such knowledge to influence others to act in ways that enhance one's personal and/or organizational objectives."[18]

Ferris' research has been confirmed through multiple studies and led to the development of the Political Skills Inventory, which includes:

- Networking ability
- Social astuteness
- Apparent sincerity
- Interpersonal influence

This makes sense when you look around you.

In a complex and changing environment like your organization, those that rise and are effective are in tune with the situation and to what matters to others (social astuteness), know who to approach for what (networking ability), and then can inspire support and trust (apparent sincerity) and/or know how to shape or direct how others act (interpersonal influence).

What's conspicuously absent as a key driver? Exactly: intelligence, hard work, technical skills. You also don't see here authenticity, positivity, transparency, or other buzzwords that pervade the popular leadership literature.

It may help to think of political skills as interpersonal skills, which many people are aware of through Daniel Goleman, who popularized the term emotional intelligence (EI), which is all about being in tune with others.[19] His research has shown that emotional intelligence accounts for nearly 90 percent of what sets high performers apart from peers with similar technical skills and knowledge. Companies he studied outperformed their goals up to 20% when senior managers there had a critical mass of EI capabilities.[20]

Emotional Intelligence consists of five components—self-awareness, self-regulation, motivation, empathy, and social skill. Many of those overlap with the political skills inventory.

If you really want to influence others and lead in organizations, you need to deal with other people, so you need that empathy and skill to understand and deal with:

- What they really want (their self-interest, their ego)
- What rubs them the wrong way (their hot buttons)
- Their identities (how they define themselves and what makes them feel good about themselves)

We'll return to these when we create a Power Map in Part II.

**True North?**

Bill George, Harvard Business School Professor and former Medtronic CEO, urges us to understand our "True North", so we can become effective and authentic leaders.

I'd argue the exact opposite.

I'd argue that it's more important to know the True North of others.

Sure, you have to have some compass of where you want to go, but if you don't know the interests of everyone around you, you're in for a heck of a time.

Of course, having power but zero internal compass can be dangerous (remember power is a means to an end). But having a true north with no power will probably result in nothing but daydreaming.

Note the Political Skills inventory, which is critical to climbing, focuses almost exclusively on your ability to read others. Even your sincerity is qualified as your "apparent sincerity."

So, do your homework and know the True North of everyone around you.

## These Principles Are Universal

Lest you believe all of this only applies to Americans and U.S. corporations, numerous studies in other countries and settings have come to similar conclusions. One study by Klaus Templer replicated the political skills research in Singapore.[21]

His findings confirmed strong workplace political skills help employees there get ahead. In fact, it helps "toxic" people rise. But two lessons from that research provoke thought: 1)

In some cases you might *want* these "toxic" personalities at the top, and 2) humble people should pay attention because those same skills that get toxic people promoted, can get the humble people promoted too.

A follow-up that summarized those findings encourages honest, humble, and hardworking people to: 1) embrace (not ignore) political skills; 2) take heed that these skills can be learned; and 3) understand that "political skills" are not necessarily "evil" or Machiavellian.[22]

Sound familiar?

To take one example: Is networking and being in tune with the needs of others evil?

## All You Need to Know About Influence

To master interpersonal influence there's only one book you need, *Influence: The Psychology of Persuasion*.[23] Robert Cialdini reviews the extensive science and research on influence, breaking down the factors of what leads people to say "yes" into six evidenced-based, universal principles:

- **Reciprocity** (we are more likely to help those who help us)

- **Scarcity** (we value more that which is hard to get, or that which we stand to lose)

- **Authority** (we follow those we perceive to be credible, knowledgeable experts)

- **Consistency** (we like to stay consistent with things we have previously said or done, so getting small commitments can lead to larger ones)

- **Liking** (we help those similar to us, who pay us compliments or make us feel good, and those who cooperate with or help us)

- **Consensus** (we look to the actions of others to determine our own)

Smart marketers have used these to great success. Technology has not changed the rules; it has only accentuated them. Quite bluntly, if you understand and apply these six principles to your interpersonal actions, your ability to influence will skyrocket.

I've trained executives and students on persuasion around the world, from sales reps in the US and Southeast Asia, to key account managers in China and Ukraine, to R&D engineers in Spain and Brazil. They are all frustrated that their logical arguments don't always win. They employ these principles and the next week "suddenly" see their accounts and projects move forward.

But I also get resistance. Some find persuasion skills "unfair" or manipulative. One professor argued I should not teach them because the CIA uses them to train agents.[24] One fellow coach called the content "manipulative bullshit." I'd argue these principles can be used for many purposes. Being close-minded doesn't help.

Another criticism, especially from engineers, is that the rules show just how confused people are–how irrational and biased we are. This is true. We make mental shortcuts to make decisions all the time. But the point they miss is that people are irrational in very predictable ways. Behavioral scientist Dan Ariely summarizes that so well in the title of his book, *Predictably Irrational*.[25] Research in social psychology and behavioral economics, dating back to Daniel Kahneman's work that won him the Nobel Prize, continue to illuminate how humans make decisions, and you should familiarize yourself with them to get ahead.

People aren't rational, so let's not pretend they are. Cialdini's six principles of influence form the basic rules of human relations.[26] These skills can be learned—and applied to effectively. And as Cialdini himself stresses, they can be applied ethically.

> **Takeaways (political skills):**
>
> There is an important and demonstrated link between political skill and career success and political skill and group performance. Having intelligence, performance, and technical skills simply isn't enough, nor is it a primary driver—and in fact, performance may not even matter. To sharpen your political skills, you need to be in tune with others, the situation, and understanding how to influence. If your political skills are not high, you can improve them by understanding, and then applying, principles of influence. People are not rational, but they are irrational in very predictable ways.

## Why Being a Great Manipulator Helps

Lest we think interpersonal skills are always warm and fuzzy, Rod Kramer gets us to consider the hard reality of "political intelligence."[27]

He shows how many top leaders are adept at finding the weak spots of others and use that information to exploit or coerce them. Doing so has helped more than one leader overcome opposition. Titans like Steve Jobs, even President Lyndon Johnson, are well known to have used this as a lever to get things done.

In fact, in situations like a rapid turnaround, you may want leaders who know how to coerce, and can move people quickly to action. Fear and loss can be a highly motivating force, more than love and gain. Research in fact shows we are loss averse, meaning we prefer to avoid loss or pain much more than if we gained the equivalent amount.[28]

So, now we know why salespeople say it is easier to sell an aspirin than a vitamin—and why Machiavelli wrote, "It is better to be feared than to be loved, if one cannot be both."

# 2. Networks and Relationships

The old adage goes "It's not what you know, it's who you know."

We are told we should network because most jobs are found through personal ties, not through advertised positions. We've all seen how knowing or having the support of an influential person can help you rise faster.

But despite this knowledge, most of us dislike networking so much that we don't do it and, therefore, seriously hurt our own prospects.

The research is stunningly clear on the benefits of networking and networks, which is why I've singled it out as a key source of power.

If you're reluctant to network, the evidence here should change your mind.

## Research on Networking Yields Surprising Insights

A longitudinal study (one that tracks the effects on people over time) by Hans-Georg Wolff and Klaus Moser of the University of Erlangen-Nuremberg showed that networking positively affects career success and salaries.[29] This lends further credence to Ferris's finding that political skills, of which networking ability is a key component, are a key driver of success.

Let's walk through the key concepts and benefits of a strong and powerful network:

**Weak Ties:** Mark Granovetter at Stanford pointed out the power of weak ties decades ago.[30] Weak ties are people you don't know deeply or don't have as much in common with. Weak ties are the opposite of strong ties, which are people you are close to, like the people in your department. This difference is best illustrated in the picture below. The dark dots are your strong ties (your tightly connected network), and the light dots are weak ties (those you are loosely connected to).

Despite its name, weak ties are actually quite powerful. Granovetter showed that weak ties are more likely to generate new information, new insights. This makes sense: Your strong ties tend to be people like you, who you spend time with, and who, by default, probably have the same information as you do. People just like you are unlikely to tell you anything you don't already know. He concluded: "Weak ties… are here seen as indispensable to individuals' opportunities."

**KEY NETWORK CONCEPTS**

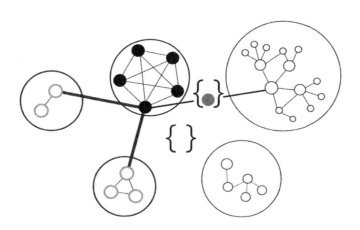

● **STRONG TIES ("BONDING")**
○— **WEAK TIES ("BRIDGING")**
{ } **STRUCTURAL HOLE**
● **BROKER ("BRIDGE HOLES")**

Weak ties are connections outside your group—people who are different, and therefore can bring *new* information, *new* insights, and *new* connections. Weak ties can lead to new thinking, innovative new ideas, and new, better jobs. This point on generating new thinking is one of the key points raised by David Epstein in his book *Range: How Generalists Triumph in a Specialized World*.[31] He reviews research that shows how generalists—those that cross boundaries and disciplines—produce more ground-breaking studies, products, innovations than their specialist peers. Making connections is a source of power.

Contrary to what you might think, weak ties, despite bringing such valuable rewards, need relatively little effort to maintain. You might, for example, only need to send a holiday note, or check in with a person every six months, to gain the benefits.

**Implication:** Think of who you spend your time with at work and outside work. Recall John the product manager who rose after his cross-functional initiative. The person in your engineering team who is connected to a venture capitalist, a journalist, or someone in consumer insights across the company, or even a divisional CEO on the rise, most likely has access to different and potentially valuable information and connections.

Having a connection or access to information is one thing—the benefit, however, comes from using it.

## Structural Holes and Brokerage Roles

Ronald Burt of the University of Chicago has conducted critical research into networks and social capital.[32] His work shows that bridging or brokering positions—or filling structural holes—are highly advantageous. Those positions, he shows, increase the odds of proposing good ideas, receiving positive evaluations and recognition, higher compensation, and faster promotions.[33,34]

Return to that chart above: Think of your work with the strong ties in dark circles as "bonding." Bonding is important when we are executing work, when we want to be a well-oiled machine. Utilizing the weak ties, to those in light circles, can be thought of as "bridging," or connecting two groups. Bridging, or brokering—if you take advantage of what the bridge offers—can bring value, and in turn make you valuable.

Take the example of John, the product manager, we saw in Chapter 4. By filling the cross-functional leadership role, John coordinated work between distinct parts of a company. We have all seen how departments and information gets "siloed" in companies, which makes those who can connect across the silos very valuable. John became the bridge, carrying the flow of information among key people, and a broker, as he found ways that distinct departments could team up and best bring the new region online (in this case by modifying an existing product that fit the market). As a result, people got to know him. He got more visibility with key stakeholders, which led to more insights—which led to the likelihood of stronger evaluations, a faster promotion, and bigger bonus than his peers.

Again, there's proof. In one of Burt's studies, he examined and compared the networks of U.S. and French executives. Those who held more bridging or brokerage roles were better connected and saw better career success. There was a clear competitive advantage to building bridge relationships and, in both countries, "resources flew disproportionately to people who provide indirect connections between otherwise disconnected groups." So, the benefits of networking, at least based on this comparison, are pretty universal.[35]

Burt also ran a field experiment, teaching executives to see social capital. Those in the company that were trained on the importance of one's position in a network—holding brokerage positions—enjoyed more success over time than those who were not exposed to the concepts. They had a control group—a group that did not receive training but otherwise equally able peers. Powerful results: Program graduates were 36–42% more likely to receive top performance evaluations, 43–72% more likely to be promoted (an effect that built in the 2 years following the program), and 42–74% were more likely to be retained by the company.[36]

What this means for you: Think of positions and jobs you take at work, where you can fill structural holes, which give you access, visibility, the opportunity to create unique value for others—and for yourself. Such activities can be as simple as leading a diverse meeting and taking and distributing the notes, to hosting a monthly series featuring external experts, to a cross-functional initiative like John took on.

## Networks vs Networking

When executives understand the importance of position, they get freed from the stereotype of networking—that you need to be an extrovert that goes to mixers and talks to everyone. In fact, that type of networking is exhausting. It's like being near a bridge and trying to meet everyone who goes across. You are better off being the person at an important toll booth—people have to come through you. You are seen as critical; you get to know what comes across first—and can choose who you engage with and how.

Albert-László Barabási of Northeastern also has a lot to say about networks. In his book *The Formula: The Universal Laws of Success,* his first law says it all: Performance does drive success, but when performance is immeasurable (which it is in most white-collar jobs), *networks determine success.*[37] And to illustrate that, he provides two graphic examples: a scientist and an artist.

You probably don't know Douglas Prasher, but he should have won the Nobel Prize for chemistry. He realized missing out was largely his own fault: He was not comfortable reaching out to people who might have helped him publish his findings. Instead, he gave the results to two of the scientists who eventually won that Nobel (news he heard years later when he was working as a van driver at a Toyota dealership).

You probably do know a starving artist, because there are many. Artists, Barabási shows, who build meaningful connections (a network) have a chance of being famous and selling expensive art in their lifetime.

Are you like Prasher or the starving artist? Barabási reminds us that life is unfair, but he doesn't care—his research focuses on understanding who succeeds and why.

## Friends in High Places: The Role of Sponsors

Finally, there's overwhelming evidence that people who get support from other powerful people ascend faster in the ranks. This has been going on informally since the beginning of time in organizations, but companies later began to formalize the process, hiring coaches, and assigning mentors and sponsors to help employees. (The nonprofit Catalyst suggests that a simple way to understand the difference between the three is that a coach talks to you, a mentor talks with you, and a sponsor talks about you.)

Think about people put on "high potential" lists or those chosen for "leadership programs". These people are trained, given executive access and support. They get more visibility and can build more relationships with those that have power. When someone with influence is aware of you, takes an interest in your growth, and advises you—they are most likely to think of you, especially when stretch roles and career-building opportunities present themselves. Getting these opportunities can further drive success.

But not everyone who advises you will be useful. Herminia Ibarra, Nancy M. Carter, and Christine Silva, drawing on a survey by Catalyst of more than 4,000 high potentials, found that more women than men had mentors, but the attention didn't translate into promotions—that instead, sponsorship was critical.[38] Because sponsors put your name forward and advocate for you behind closed doors, they are a much more massive career accelerator. Economist Sylvia Ann Hewlett summarized it best in the title of her book: *Forget a Mentor, Find A Sponsor: The New Way to Fast-Track Your Career.*[39] Sponsors really promote you.

Indeed, McKinsey, numerous academics, and Catalyst have found that a lack of sponsors is one of the major deterrents to women and minorities rising.[40] One study, led by Yang Yang, found that a strong network and female-dominated inner circle highly benefited women: They had an expected job placement level 2.5 times greater than women with few connections and a male-dominated inner circle.[41]

It's unlikely your company has a formal sponsorship program, so take fate into your own hands and work on obtaining one.

## Building a Better Network

You need to be proactive in building your network and refreshing it often. The problem most of us have is we stay in our strong ties group, move in the same social circles—people similar to us—which becomes an echo chamber. We then can get pigeonholed as others can't see you doing something different, or get myopic, seeing only what is in front of us.

Research on network advantage by Herminia Ibarra of London Business School[42] helps you do this and ties the concepts we have seen together. She has shown that strong, effective networks depend on three qualities:

- **Breadth** - strong relationships with diverse contacts (weak ties). Include people inside and outside your organization, of different backgrounds, and different levels.

- **Connectivity** - the capacity to link or bridge across separate groups (bridging and brokering). Find positions and people that are super connectors, people who can open up even more channels.

- **Dynamism** - having a set of extended ties that evolves and is not just backward looking. Refresh your network: periodically adding new blood to your network is needed.

Keep these three points in mind as you audit your current network and plan how to strengthen it. Then act.

**Takeaways (network and relationships):**

Building a strong network is not just about being extroverted and going to random mixers. You need to be strategic and deliberate to create a network that has breadth (weak ties), connectivity (enabling you to broker structural holes), and dynamism (will keep refreshing your network). That executive you dismissed, who sits on diverse committees, meets people outside the department and company regularly and has created their own diverse personal board of advisors (coaches, mentors, sponsors) is probably spending their time more wisely than you think. So, audit your network, and take action as your career growth greatly depends on it.

## The value of a strong network is... universal

I spent a large part of my business career in China, and the Chinese liked to say the key to success there was your 关系 - guanxi. "Guanxi" translates as your social relationships, your network—personal ties that help you out.

What annoyed me was hearing Chinese and western executives talk about it like some mysterious, un-knowable force—that was China specific.

Because the word guanxi comes up so often when discussing China, I always had to explain the concept in a course I taught on China to MBA students at IE Business School in Spain. After explaining what guanxi meant, I smiled: a half a dozen students, all from different countries, said, "This is the same in my country—in fact, we have a word for it."

Years later, Ron Burt and colleagues examined just how important guanxi was to the success of Chinese entrepreneurs. Guanxi, they found, provided information, powerful ties, and support. Being strategically connected (broker networks) in China correlated to business success—the same conclusion they had reached in research conducted in the US and Europe.

So, yes, guanxi and the power of networks is alive and well, everywhere.

## 3. Visibility and Brand

Unfortunately, we don't give ourselves a promotion. Other people do, and those who do generally are people in higher positions, with power.

More harsh news for you: Powerful people are thinking about you far less than you think.

Do the people who can promote you know who you are? Do they know what you contribute?

The basic rule in marketing is that your product will not be purchased if people don't know about it, don't uniquely associate it with something they need or want, and don't know where to find it. The same is true for you: People cannot promote what they do not know and cannot recall.

If you perform well, but no one knows about it, you might be like the tree that falls in the forest. Why leave that solely to chance? The chances are that someone else might be taking credit for it. Or even if they don't take credit, maybe they are given credit. Research shows that in group work, one individual is usually attributed by others as being the primary driver.

Think about a simple PIE chart. There's your Performance, Image, and Exposure. You need all three, but most people focus only on performance.

Recall John the product manager, and what he gained when he started giving bi-weekly updates with the CEO and engaged with key stakeholders across the firm. If you forge strong networks, you get visibility as well. And if you do good things, and people talk about them to others, you create a powerful, known brand.

## What's Your Brand?

What do other people say about you when you are not in the room?

That's my definition of brand.

What adjectives come to mind when your name comes up?

It is essential for you to know this information and to take an active role in shaping your brand reputation. Ask others (directly, if you feel they are willing to be honest) or seek 360 feedback, something many organizations conduct regularly and a tool I use in my coaching practice.

It's important to know if you see yourself in one way—for example as a leader—but no one else does. This happened to one of my clients, whose two bosses told me, in separate 360 reviews, "She just doesn't show up like a leader. She shows up with updates, like she was reporting the weather—and not with recommendations and insight."

Pay attention to how you talk about and define yourself. One executive I worked with was overly deferential and thought being funny was his superpower, but 360 reviews showed that top leaders were wary of promoting him because he "wasn't confident or serious enough," two criteria they demanded of the leadership team.

Dorie Clark, in her books *Reinventing You* and *Stand Out*, masterfully breaks down what it takes to build a strong personal brand and have visibility. Clark wants good people to succeed, and not to fade into obscurity, like Douglas Prasher the chemist did.

She herself—and the many people she coaches and teaches—demonstrate the core principles you need if you want to stand out:[43]

- **Differentiation:** Being different is better than being better (differentiation cuts through the noise and gets remembered). Everyone has a unique story, so tell it. Furthermore, the simpler and less complicated you make it, the better. Research shows our minds can't hold more than a few ideas before we go into confusion and overload from thinking too much.[44]

- **Social Proof:** If you recall Cialdini's principles of influence, we look for mental shortcuts to help us determine if someone is credible. Prestigious affiliations, connections, honors can do just that. This is why influencer or third-party endorsements are so highly sought after and paid for—and even when they are false, they can still create a reputation.[45]

- **Exposure:** Think about being exposed to an advertisement—that used to come via direct mail, radio and TV, then email and now through social media. Research shows exposure, or repetition, works and aids recall. In fact, the "mere exposure effect" shows that the more we are exposed to something, the more it sinks in.[46] We can become accustomed to it or even start to like it—even if it is something we don't particularly care for.

You need to own a position in the mind of those that matter. This, of course, is nothing new, just re-read the classic *Positioning: The Battle for Your Mind* by Jack Trout and Al Ries.[47] While the tools may have changed since they wrote their classic, the principles certainly have not.

Clark shows how content generation and an active following, or community of followers, work together and amplify each other, especially on social media, due to network effects. Indeed, she argues, in a free agent economy, having your own brand may not only be powerful—but essential. The rewards for being recognized are substantial, leading to higher paying opportunities. Barabási, the network scholar and author of *The Formula: The Universal Laws of Success*, shows this in his Law #2 ("performance is bounded but success is unbounded"). Those who rise to #1 get wildly disproportionate rewards, dwarfing even those in second place.

Personal brand and reputation management have become so important that top schools have integrated it into their offerings, like at Stanford where Allison Kluger and Supermodel Tyra Banks teach one such class.

## Be Strategic in Your Brand Building

You want to be strategic about the brand you build. Will it help you, bring value, get you where you want to go?

If you don't like your existing brand, shape it! Change how you talk about your past, and your present. Barabási's third law of success: "Future success can get a boost from even the perception of past success." That points to the importance of creating that aura. Amping yourself up and looking the part is critical.

And that's exactly what one executive I coached did. Wanting to move into strategy and become less known as a data cruncher, he shifted how he spoke about himself. He started to delegate his data-related tasks to his team and then actively spoke about strategy in key meetings. He recast past work he had done in more strategic terms, omitting the executional part. He removed many analytical skills from his profile and resume. Consistently doing this over time shifted how people thought about him, something we tracked by how many senior executives started to seek his strategic advice. That eventually led to a conversation with the company's president, who wanted to tap him to head up the company's entry into a new area.

Another client took that idea a step further. He created an internal podcast, teaming up with a head in marketing. He interviewed top leaders across his division, asking them 3 questions. This got him visibility with all those leaders, but also softened his reputation. In reviews, people found him rigid, something leaders told me they worried about and why he had not been promoted. On episode after episode, he showed a charming side. Perception of him changed rapidly.

What do you want people to say about you? Ron Burt, the expert on brokerage, studies how gossip and chatter have an important impact on workplace reputations. Are you memorable? Do stories about you travel to more than five people? Or are you the person who is dead at their desk for five days and no one knows?

Perception, as they say, can be everything. And that brings us to the next point: how you show up.

**Takeaways (Visibility and Brand):**

You should carefully cultivate and manage your visibility and brand. Think about a PIE chart and make sure you are not only Performing but tending to your Image and Exposure. Don't assume people know you because it's quite possible someone else is taking credit or being given credit for what you do. Not only are the potential rewards high in your company, but a strong brand can bring you job offers and accolades which increase your power, or leverage, with your employer. They can also accelerate your success if you go independent.

## 4. Executive Presence and Communication Skills

Ever experience any of the following:

- You said something in a meeting… only to have someone else say the same thing later, to which the boss says to the speaker, "Amazing point! Great work!"
- You left a speech inspired and enthused, but don't remember what was even said?
- You had a peer who does not know the details, but somehow convinces all the higher ups in the room of the plan's greatness?
- You heard, like I have in 360 reviews I conduct for clients, "Well, Pat just doesn't show up and act like a leader."

If so, you are not alone. My clients mention them all the time.

And if you have experienced them, you see the powerful impact of Executive Presence and Communication.

Performance and hard work might get you recognized, but "leadership potential" isn't enough to get you into the executive suite, according to the Center for Talent Innovation. Their research, conducted with nearly 4,000 professionals, showed that leadership roles are given to those who also *look and act the part*.[48]

Sylvia Ann Hewlett, co-sponsor of the research and author of
*EP*, breaks down Executive Presence—a widely talked about
but poorly understand topic—into three pillars:

- **Appearance** (attire, grooming, and
  physical attractiveness)

- **Communication** (speaking skills, the ability to
  command and read a room)

- **Gravitas** (exuding grace under fire, projecting vision)

While not all these factors accelerate promotions, lack of
them can deter your chances, the survey stresses.

Let's unpack each.

## It's All Subjective—and Unjust

## Appearance

Research at Princeton and Stanford shows we make snap
judgments about people within the first 5-10 milliseconds,
even before they open their mouth—and those judgements
are remarkably sticky and hold over time.[49] That's what
they found when they had students evaluate professors:
Judgements made about a professor's competence in those
first seconds remained remarkably stable through the entire
semester.

So, first impressions matter—a lot.

There is an unjust side here, to be sure: Handsome people, tall people, or white men may be unfairly seen—due to implicit bias, linked to stereotypes—as more competent, which is associated with power and leadership qualities.

But what can we control? Dress and our body language, for one. This feels like a no-brainer, but many people fail to pay attention to it. Even during the pandemic when connecting remotely via video, I pointed out to two clients how arriving unkempt, in a t-shirt with a messy bedroom in the backdrop, was probably not setting the ideal impression with senior management.

Pay close attention to that backdrop and how you show up. A good case to study is Eric Adams, the mayor of New York, who pays a lot of attention to what he wears and strongly advises others to do so as well. He uses his dress to symbolize what he stands for, to connect, and differentiate—to build his brand.[50] It is true, a picture is worth a thousand words. "People look at your presentation before they take you seriously," he says. "Everything about you must say power."

Research also shows that impressions may be set *even before you show up*. It turns out there is evidence supporting the use of inspirational music, a powerful image as a backdrop, spraying fragrances, or posing questions in advance: These cues can predispose us, or "pre-suade" us toward a desired result, according to Robert Cialdini.[51] It's influence in another form, an area in the social sciences called priming, that should make you think twice about where you present, who proceeds you, or actions you might take with the audience, even before a meeting starts.

## Can I reverse a bad first impression?

If impressions are set immediately—and hold strongly over time—many people worry that they are powerless to reverse a poor impression. It's true you don't get a second chance to make a first impression, but that doesn't mean your relationship with someone is fixed forever.

**Steps you can take:**

**Ask yourself, does this person really matter?:** We often get caught in minor tiffs or want to be liked by everyone. If the other person is not on your critical path, let it go.

**Validate your impression is correct:** Don't assume. Maybe the other person dismissed your idea that day because they had a fight with their child right before the meeting. Be a bit of a detective, ask others you trust, maybe ask that person directly.

**Be curious:** If it seems a negative impression was set, take the other person's position and think about what may have made them upset. How might you have contributed to the problem? Maybe you criticized them in front of their boss and were disrespectful in some way. If you get a sense of what set the bad impression, you are more likely to be able to correct it.

**"Re-set" the relationship:** Speaking 1-1 about it, exploring or owning what you may have done, can help—maybe there was context the other person did not see. Also consider re-direction: focusing the cause on something external to the two of you, to de-personalize things.

**Enlist others to help:** You need strong allies and supporters across the company. As the Power Map will reveal, allies can provide information or influence people in ways that you directly cannot.

**Follow-through and do, repeatedly, in ways that are seen:** If you've identified what you need to do to change someone's mind, follow through and model that behavior, in ways that are visible. If showing up late to an initial meeting set the person off, doing it again is a surefire way to make the situation worse.

**Build your own power:** The best defense is often a good offense. If you have a blocking boss, you need to build power around them. The more power you build, the less someone else can get in your way.

**Cut bait:** Sometimes it's not worth the effort to reverse a deeply set impression. You might be better off leaving if things are bad, like making a lateral move or looking outside the organization.

**Some people are real jerks, so get away from them:** With assholes, it's best to maintain distance lest you get sucked into their energy. All the more reason to build your own power or shift to a new position.

**Communication (your speaking skills, your ability to "command a room")**

What good is your speech if no one remembers the key idea, or takes action?

The ability to be clear and persuasive is often deemed the most important—but also the most harshly judged—leadership skill. So, how you present yourself and share your ideas is critical.

Research shows that we pay disproportionate attention to nonverbal communication, especially when someone's body language and spoken words don't agree.[52] So, you should probably pay more time and attention to body language and tone of voice, instead of another three hours formatting your PowerPoint slides.

When you do present information, the classic mistake is to present too much. Research shows people can hold at best three ideas and then go into overload. So, think about subtracting, instead of adding.

Less is more—and how we present that information can have a dramatic effect on what people actually retain. Chip and Dan Health, in their bestseller *Made to Stick*, distill evidenced-based research into their SUCCESS model of high impact communication.[53] That Model: Ideas that stick are Simple, Unexpected, Concrete, Credible, Emotional, and Stories. They show, for example, how stories are retained significantly more than numbers, that the use of familiar analogies has the best chance of helping people understand complex ideas.

Furthermore, people retain structured information up to 40% more reliably and accurately than information presented in a free form manner.[54] That's one reason communication coach Matt Abrahams recommends structures such as, past-present-future; problem-solution-benefit; or what? - so what? - now what?

Finally, a host of small words—using "em's" and "uh's," and hedging words such as, "I think," "I believe" "possibly", often undercut the messenger. Lacing your speech with hedging words, according to linguist Deborah Tannen, can unwittingly lead others to see you as lacking conviction and confidence.[55]

**Gravitas (exuding grace under fire, projecting vision)**

This brings us to the last pillar. People are predisposed to believing a single powerful person can hold the key and answer to their problems. This has historically been called the "great man theory," and explains why leadership programs that stress the "shadow of the leader" sell so well.

As Julie Battilana and Tiziana Casciaro write, political scientists have shown that "many of us, across cultures, are disposed to prefer people who project an air of strength and sense of supreme control, people who give us a feeling of security and stability."[56] We, therefore, falsely attribute one's persona and aura to competence. That's why Margarita Mayo writes that we fall for so many charismatic narcissistic leaders, and Tomas Chamorro-Premuzic believes so many incompetent men become leaders.[57]

Indeed, gravitas is the hardest part of executive presence to get a handle on.

But there's research that can help us understand it—and even build it.

Contrary to common wisdom, communicating charismatically and with impact can be learned. In studies on how leaders are perceived in their communication, John Antonakis at IMD Business School, identified a dozen key CLTs (charismatic leadership tactics).[58]

These CLTs included nine verbal tactics—using metaphors, analogies, stories, three-part lists, among others; and three non-verbal tactics: animated face, gestures, and facial expressions. After executives trained on these tactics, their leadership rating observers gave them rose by about 60%.

People who sound more definitive are seen as more powerful and confident—qualities for better or worse—we want to see in leaders.

## Acting the Part

The late Harriet Rubin, who worked with some of the great CEOs in history, observed that the secret to leadership often had to do with "pretense, playing a role, and the theatrical arts."[59] She went further to point out that sometimes they were at their powers when they were not their authentic selves—that they had the ability to inspire confidence.

If your company goes through a crisis, you can see why this is important. Your job as a leader is to pull people through—and ensure people take the necessary actions. If you show up and say you have no idea what is going on (quite likely your authentic response), you are likely to lose the confidence of others, particularly those like your boss or board that keep you in power. Sitting on the sidelines is not a place where you can affect much change.

Rubin summed it up: "The message: Act powerful and you become powerful." That may sound like a sound bite, but there is evidence in this area as well.

Social scientists have found that being put in the right frame of mind can activate how powerfully and confidently you show up. In one study, led by Joris Lammers, researchers found that people who read powerful stories right before they went into job interviews were accepted more than twice as much as the group who had not read stories in advance.[60] Why? Those "primed" with power displayed greater confidence and were thus viewed as more capable and competent.

These small changes in mindset—even activated by thinking about a prior experience when one had power—can also alter behavior, including increasing one's willingness to take action.[61] So, thinking of yourself as powerful can make you powerful.

This "priming" of power can occur in other ways as well. Dana Carney and Amy Cuddy found that doing "power poses" (think of a confident hands-on-hip Wonder Woman or Superman pose) increased one's physiological response levels—and behavior. High "power posers" experienced elevations in testosterone, a decrease in cortisol, and increased feelings of power and risk."[62] This finding led legions of people to "power pose" before important presentations and job interviews. It turns out you may be able to fake it—and become it.

The downside of feeling more powerful, however, is it can lead to overconfidence, arrogance, and loss of perspective, which can lead to risk-seeking, reckless behavior and lead to poor decisions.[63] That's something we will look at how to manage later in the book—but it does not mean we should ignore the power priming research. Priming yourself may help us to act more powerfully, in moments when we might benefit from it—like when John the product manager needed to show up and present more convincingly to the C-Suite.

## To Be or Not to Be

The idea that leadership is a lot about acting is one of the reasons why Deb Gruenfeld's course at Stanford, "Acting with Power," is so in demand. In her latest book she draws lessons from research and acting that allow us to become powerful.[64] Expansive body language, tone, and cadence can help us project and feel more powerful—skills actors train on intensely. Many actors in fact "prime" themselves right before they get into a role, by recalling a particular event or story.

All of this is not to say that power implies being forceful. Executive coach Ed Batista, drawing from clips of the Godfather, shows how we often confuse force and power.[65] Subtle hand gestures or ways in which we control conversations—like prolonged silence—can be highly effective and elevate our status.

> **Takeaways (executive presence and communication skills):**
>
> "Be yourself up there" is shallow and not so productive advice. Remember that it's not what you say, but what other people perceive and take away. How you show up, how you act, and how you carry yourself matters more than we care to admit since first impressions are set within seconds—and can carry on over time. The next time you prepare for a presentation, spend time on the setting, your body language and tone, and how you structure the information and message—it might be much more important than the actual content! Finally, think like an actor. Priming yourself, by reading a powerful story, recalling a time you were powerful, or by doing power poses, may get you "into the role". Ultimately, you can develop presence and become a sharper communicator—if you pay attention to the research and then apply it. Practice and get feedback, even videotape and watch yourself to catch bad habits. Doing so, your presence, communication, confidence and, ultimately you, will rise.

## Learn from Kate Winslet

Actors have to get into roles; it's what they do for a living. So, if leadership is a lot about acting, we should be able to learn a lot from them.

Here's what great actors do, that you can to:

1) **They study the role:** What is the background, situation, context? This helps them mentally prepare.
2) **They get in the role:** Often, right before the camera rolls, they "prime" themselves by recounting a moment or story to put them in the frame of mind needed.
3) **They practice and get feedback:** The great actors and actresses are insane about getting feedback from coaches, directors—or reviewing recordings of themselves. It's that process called deliberate practice.

I took great interest in how British actress Kate Winslet nailed the "Delco" accent in the HBO hit series, *Mare of Easttown*. (Because that is the area where I grew up, and an accent I immediately recognize). The accent is viewed as one of the hardest to master.

Her not so hidden secret? The three things listed above.

## 5. Control of Hard Resources

I'm not going to spend a lot of time on this topic. It's pretty obvious that if you control key things (for example: budget, veto power, the right to hire and fire people), you can wield immense power. It gives you the power to grant favors or mete out punishments. Using them repeatedly can then send signals.

For all our talk of soft power, there is nothing like hard power. That's not to say people will always listen, nor should it be your only tool, but just look at dictators. In fact, *The Dictator's Handbook: Why Bad Behavior is Almost Always Good Politics*, by political scientists Bruce Bueno de Mesquita and Alastair Smith, convincingly shows how tyrants and democrats grow and hold power and authority using the same principles.[66]

**Sometimes you want a slingshot–sometimes the spear:**

Think about David in the story of David and Goliath. The very absence of size and a big spear forced David to come up with other solutions, using his slingshot to eventually win the day. He turned his disadvantage into an advantage.

As one of my clients, a project manager, complained: "My job is like herding cats, who don't want to be herded. I've learned to read people well, build an arsenal of techniques. I know how to nudge them and be a pied piper, but it can be exhausting. Sometimes I wish I controlled a bag of treats they really liked, and it wouldn't hurt to have an electric shocker too."

Project managers, because they are deprived of hard sources of power (a budget, dedicated reports, for example), get really good at mastering influence. If they don't, they fail. It becomes a source of power.

But the message here runs deeper.

Sometimes you want the spear. We all know there is nothing like hard control and stronger authority (although just because you have it, doesn't always mean people will listen to you, and doesn't always mean you will win). Don't forget that hard power is a source of power.

David would be most powerful if he had not only his slingshot but also the spear. Goliath would also have been more powerful if he had both weapons.

The message: Expand your toolkit, and you'll be better off. The advantages of control over hard resources are obvious. Don't be shy about obtaining them—and using them.

# A Final Word: Personal Qualities and Attributes

There's no doubt that certain personal qualities, or attributes, can be additional sources of power. Most of those qualities relevant to building power, however, have overlap with strong political and interpersonal skills (being attuned to others, networking or making connections, influence skills).

But I want to comment on three buckets of personal qualities, which my clients ask about, probably because these surface in corporate assessments, performance reviews—and uncomfortable conversations. These buckets are related to our motivations, our "will" and "skill", and our physical appearance.

## Motivations

Sometimes I hear in a 360 review, "S/he just doesn't have the drive or desire." To state the obvious, if you're not motivated to rise and lead in your organization, it's unlikely you will.

Indeed, people have different motivations at work. One study looked at the motivations of managers and their professional success.[67]

Three groups were compared:

1. Those motivated for affiliation (being liked).
2. Those motivated for achievement.
3. Those motivated by power.

The third group, those most interested in power, achieved greater positions of influence—which should make you ask yourself how you feel about power.

## Will and Skill

The Will vs Skill matrix, which has roots in Ken Blanchard's situational leadership model and was popularized in the *Tao of Coaching* by Max Landsberg, remains every manager's favorite tool. "Will" looks at desire or motivation, and "skill" the ability to make things happen.

In regard to what builds power, Jeff Pfeffer, drawing from research and leaders he has studied, focuses on seven personal qualities.[68] Will derives from ambition, energy, and focus. Skill derives from self-knowledge, confidence, empathy, and the ability to tolerate conflict. Note the absence of raw intelligence—which he believes, and the research we've looked at suggests, is highly overrated.

To this list, I add one important quality: persistence. Albert-László Barabási of Northeastern University has shown that success can come at any time—as long as we are persistent.

The vital question is whether you believe these personal qualities can be developed. While one's ambitions may be a personal choice, research and my coaching practice would suggest they all definitely can be developed. Take empathy. Research shows we can increase our empathy by spending time with other people (so you "walk in their shoes"), or even through deliberate exercises, like considering another person's perspective and potential reactions, before you take action.

In order to develop these qualities, however, you need to accurately understand yourself, your strengths and weaknesses. Self-knowledge can come from observation and self-reflection, through activities like journaling. It can also come from feedback, directly from others or through assessment mechanisms like 360 reviews. That's why both of these practices are ideally integrated into most coaching engagements.

As you think about the personal qualities, consider that being too strong in any given dimension can hurt you. Return to empathy. Too little and you may miss what's important to a key stakeholder. But too much and you may take the other side's feelings too much into account. Trying to please everyone, you can get paralyzed or become overly acquiescent and accommodating (becoming that doormat).

**Physical Traits**

People sometimes ask if physical, or innate traits like one's appearance help build power. (They usually ask this after hearing that CEOs tend to be taller or more handsome than the average population.)

As we saw in the discussion on executive presence, because we make snap judgments, appearance can often give a status boost (perhaps a taller, fit person is perceived as having their act together and therefore is seen as "strong" and therefore competent). At the same time, women or minorities may get penalized—get a decrease in status—due to prevailing stereotypes and implicit biases we hold. Because your gender, race, and even other traits can't be changed, we've entered an important topic—one that we will examine more deeply in the next chapter.

**Takeaways (personal qualities and attributes):**

Personal qualities that build power can derive from your will (your motivation - ambition, energy, and focus) and skill (your ability to make things happen - self-knowledge, confidence, empathy, and the ability to tolerate conflict.) These are not innate traits but can be developed through self-reflection, feedback, practice—and dogged persistence. Taking the steps to do so (which is why you picked up this book) will grow your power. It's never too late. Traits that may be innate, like physical appearance, gender or race, may also affect status and the way we are received, due the fact we make snap judgments, some of which may be based on prevailing stereotypes. Because these traits generally cannot be changed, we need to understand how they operate and their impact, a topic addressed in the next chapter.

# CHAPTER 6

# Truths We Would Rather Ignore

This final section exploring the research and evidence covers two areas:

1) Under-examined aspects of communication—anger, interruption, not apologizing and framing information—that are often dismissed because of their negative associations.
2) Challenges that women, minorities and other historically marginalized groups face—and how to address so-called "double-binds."

If you don't want to read the evidence, you can go straight to the "Takeaways" section highlighted at the end of each section.

## Under-Examined Aspects of Communication

At the end of the previous chapter, we covered effective communication techniques. Many executives have been exposed to these in communication and public speaking courses. The evidence backing those prescriptions is generally acknowledged.

The concepts I share next, however, are widely reviled—despite strong evidence showing how they can be effective.

Contrary to what we want to believe and are told, power can also be built by displaying anger, interrupting and being critical, *not* apologizing—and how we frame or share information. They are underutilized and can confer many advantages.

Before throwing out the baby with the bath water, hear me out:

## Anger

We are raised and taught to suppress anger, but research has shown that displays of anger can boost our status, and that we perceive angry people as strong. Strength signals confidence, which often is equated with competence.

There's also evidence that expressing anger can be more powerful than showing sadness or remorse.[69] While we may like people who show sadness and contrition, we confer lower status on them. When Bill Clinton testified during the Monica Lewinsky scandal years back, research showed that people viewed his initial apology and remorse as humble and warm but conferred lower status to him.[70] When he went on the offensive and got angry, he was found less likable, but his status improved. Barack Obama has been famously lampooned for his composed, rather than fiery, approach.[71]

Anger can indicate you mean business, which may get your adversaries to think twice before confronting you—or get others to rally behind you. You may dislike Donald Trump, Devin Nunes, Elise Stefanik, Kamala Harris, Elizabeth Warren, and Bernie Sanders, but their displays of toughness and ire make them formidable figures.

This does not mean, however, that you should fly off the handle and start banging a table and yelling. Anger can be difficult to control, and studies have shown that extreme anger may backfire while moderate anger does boost status.[72]

In summary, we may not like angry people, but we often see them as powerful and competent, which means we may let them get their way—and that may be a lever you wish to use to get things done. So, the next time your impulse is to avoid anger, take a step back and think how channeling it strategically might be seen as a leadership strength.[73]

## Interrupting and Being Critical

The same argument holds for people who interrupt or are critical. Powerful people, because they tend to be less inhibited, feel freer to interrupt. So interrupting, while it may feel rude, can also be a sign of your power.

Experiments found that when three experts evaluated a paper, the expert that was critical of the conclusions was perceived as more competent than two other experts, who were not critical.

Again, read your situation, but the evidence suggests that always being silent and never sharing an opinion can have unintended consequences. Remember Sam, the brand manager we saw in Chapter 3? Executives interpreted her silence as meaning she was unsure or unwilling to defend a point of view.

## Not Apologizing

I often have clients ask me, "I worry that apologizing will make me look weak."

We believe the right and moral thing is to apologize when we have done wrong. But these clients are right to be concerned: Apologies are incredibly difficult to get right, and studies have shown that we consistently overestimate the positive impact our apologies will have.[74]

On top of that, many people over-apologize. Gratuitous apologies, "Sorry I'm two minutes late" or "Oh, that is my fault" can have the unintended consequence of lowering our status. Apologizing too much and repeatedly brings even more attention to that fact, and taking full blame for something that is not entirely your fault can lead you to become the fall guy.

Most worrisome is that there seems to be very little penalty for *not apologizing*. Moral considerations aside, Cass Sunstein demonstrates quite convincingly that "In politics, apologies are for losers."[75] The same can be said for corporate apologies.[76] Those that deflect and not apologize tend to get off, without penalty, and continue in power. While those that own up, lose their status and positions—and get sidelined.

As such, *not* apologizing is an under-examined strategy, especially since delivering an effective apology that still keeps you in a position to get things done is so hard to do well. And that brings us to the final controversial arena.

## Framing

Behavioral scientist Dan Ariely, in his book *The (Honest) Truth About Dishonesty*, shows how we frequently bend the truth and when lying serves us—and how understanding these insights can help us.

Consider how saying something nice about someone you detest (a small "white lie") might put them in a better mood. In some situations, this may be necessary and indeed helpful. After all, you don't always get to choose your peers at work and may need to work with them.

Think about what you choose to say, how you say it, and where you focus the spotlight—how you "frame" information. Bending the truth and redirection, or as Jeff Pfeffer sometimes describes it, "strategic misrepresentation," is widely used—and can be very effective.

Where you put people's attention can make all the difference. Refocusing attention on another topic can shift the focus entirely. There are few objective facts—even numbers lie, and people manipulate how they are presented all the time...

We have already discussed how apologies can make you look weak and cost you your support and job—so think about how reframing a situation can help. For example, reframe an oversight as a learning. Rather than dwell on a tragedy and mishap, acknowledge it, focus more attention on the rapid response or on your certainty that things will get better. Rather than be the fall guy, own your small piece but call attention to the wider responsibility of the organization and the deeper implications.

In these examples, are you lying? How you frame and "manage the narrative" can make all the difference.

> **Takeaways (anger and other under-examined aspects of communication):**
>
> Our knee-jerk response is that only jackasses and bullies would get angry, interrupt and criticize, fail to apologize, or blatantly bend the truth. But take a moment to examine the evidence and observe your own organization. These strategies can boost status, build power, or serve you in managing key relationships and getting things done. Channeling them, in the right moments, may be a valuable tool to round out your toolbox—or quite possibly save your career.

## Challenges that Women (and Other Groups) Face

*"I've been told by my boss that I'm 'knocking it out of the park' and take great care of my team… but because I am warm and empathetic, he says I'm not being 'tough enough'*

*or making unpopular calls because he believes I'm worried about protecting my image as 'best boss.' The leaders in my organization say I need to show up more decisively, and with authority, if I want to rise to the VP level... but when I do exactly that (in fact copying behaviors I see), I get told I am bossy, aggressive, and that I turn people off.*

*When my white male peers do the same thing, they are seen as leaders... When I do it, I'm called a bitch, and may even get penalized or backlash—like being passed over for the promotion. What does it take? Do I have to fire someone, which seems like a rash and unwise action, just to show I've got what it takes?*

*Feels like darned if I do, doomed if I don't.*

*What am I supposed to do?"*

- Lisa, senior executive and client of mine,
Fortune 500 multinational

I've heard Lisa's dilemma repeated over and over, from other women, minorities, or those who represent historically marginalized groups in their countries or companies.

Let's first state the obvious: The world is not fair. Women continue to be paid less than men, and the advancement of women and minorities into senior ranks, around the globe, remains slow. You'd have to have your head in the sand to say the playing field is level. It's not.

Research and figures have highlighted the challenges:

- Victoria Brescoll, in her research on perceptions of emotion in the workplace, asked bluntly: "Can an angry woman get ahead?"[77]
- A survey on the career progress of Asian-Americans in the U.S. by the Ascend Foundation, stated it directly: "Asians are the first to be hired, and last to be promoted."[78] And research in North America revealed that when East Asian men and women violated stereotypes, like appearing more dominant, they received more harassment at work, compared to other employee groups.[79]
- Studies led by the sociologist Robert Livingston found that Black men with non-threatening "baby faces" were more likely to be CEOs, than their more threatening-faced Black peers. Yet Black women who were forceful and expressed dominance got a status boost—similar to the boost white men gained.[80]

That's more than enough to make your head spin—and scrutinize every action you take at work, like Lisa was doing. It would be great if we could "just be ourself" or follow one simple prescription of what to do to get ahead. But it's clearly not that easy.

## So, What Is Lisa Supposed to Do?

What do we do about bias? Do these findings mean the sources of power won't work to build power for her, or other groups?

In her own words:

> *"I know the world is not fair—that there are inequity and systemic problems that need to be changed. I back moves to make that happen... but they are not going to happen overnight. I also don't want to play the woman or bias card, or complain… I have spent my life working hard, rising to every challenge put in front of me, earned everything I have accomplished—and I respect the chain of command. But there are definitely some double standards here.*
>
> *I want some actionable strategies that will work for me, today. In the next year, I know I will have missed the window to get promoted."*

Here are 6 considerations and practical strategies, ones that are drawn from research and have shown to be the most effective for my clients:

## 1) Remember That Theories of Power Are Universal

Numerous studies have shown that theories of power hold across time and contexts, for example:[81]

- It's almost a law of human nature that we form into hierarchies, we like others similar to ourselves, and we help those that make us feel good about ourselves.
- The political skills inventory, the principles of influence, and the advantages gained from one's position in a network have been replicated with diverse groups, in multiple geographies.

- Beliefs about the non-verbal expression of social power have been shown to be consistent across genders.
- And numerous studies have found that many well-known gender differences can be reproduced by manipulating power—that is to say men and women gain similarly from "power priming," and that gender differences reflect power differences.

The key message: Theories of power are sound, so don't throw out the baby with the bathwater. Don't revert to those feel-good prescriptions of what authentic leaders should do, which is totally untethered from reality!

## 2) Adjust Your Strategy, Based on the Situation

Because people gravitate to others like themselves, people in powerful positions are predisposed to reward styles similar to themselves. By extension, they may not reward styles that clash with their styles.[82] You need to understand how the dominant group in power and prevailing norms operate. You need to take this into account when planning how to build power.

In plain English: It's not a one-size-fits-all approach to building power. You need to adjust strategies you use—but that doesn't mean throwing the playbook to build power out the window.

You adjust your strategies (how you build power), based on the situation (for example the culture or the context or stereotypes and biases that may be in play).

This is a critical but nuanced point, that Inbal Demri states very well: The key to advancing is to *use the information we know about power—and the information we know about bias (or context)*—to help us select the optimal strategies to deploy and hopefully avoid ones less likely to succeed.[83]

Two simple examples to illustrate the point in practice:

- An American male manager might build his network more casually, perhaps reaching out directly to make a connection, because of the informal culture in U.S. society. A French male manager might build his network following more protocol because of tighter cultural rules. A Brazilian woman manager might build her network through social ties, reflecting cultural or gender norms there.[84] These are differences in approach to building a network—but it doesn't change the fact that in all three cases, gaining that key brokerage position in the network and building a diverse, connective and dynamic network (Source of Power #2) is most beneficial.
- A man who gets angry may be seen as confident and leader-like. But a woman, because of the stereotype that she is supposed to be warm and caring, should tread carefully displaying that same raw anger. This doesn't change the fact that we want to see "strong" behaviors in our leaders, which can signal competence. If a woman is seen as less competent for being wildly angry, she might adjust her approach: show a stern look or use a forceful hand gesture or direct her anger at a larger cause (a way she can show

commitment and caring, without being attacking), or have influential allies validate or support her when she channels her ire.

The takeaway is to adjust, reading the situation—and incorporate what we understand about power and bias.

### 3) Apply "Judo" to Turn a Perceived Weakness into a Strength)

Joan Williams at the University of California encourages us to apply "gender judo" to address the double-bind women face, providing a practical way we can adjust strategies to account for bias.[85]

The sport of judo is about taking your opponent's momentum and using it against him or her. Gender judo takes feminine stereotypes that can hold women back in the workplace and turns them around, to forge ahead.

An example would be a woman negotiating her salary. Because women typically don't ask or assert, and men do, men have been shown to negotiate better bumps in salary negotiations. But when a woman asks, she may get penalized for being brash and rude, because she is violating a stereotype of women as nurturing and passive. Gender judo here would involve a woman asking but positioning her request like she is negotiating for the team, rather than herself. That's taking a stereotypically feminine strength (caring) but marrying it with a traditionally masculine trait (assertion) to get the desired result.

It sucks that we have to think this deeply. And this strategy may upset some, as it panders to stereotypes. But 1) it works, and 2) it may be the most practical, actionable strategy we have at the moment. Navigating bias isn't the same as eliminating it, which requires deeper structural changes that are unlikely to happen anytime soon.

Applying judo can work for more than women. It has also been around: Recall Ronald Reagan's classic line in his debate with Walter Mondale, "I am not going to exploit, for political purposes, my opponent's youth and inexperience." He took a perceived weakness and turned it into a strength. Many of my clients who are not women, in fact, have applied this framework artfully to succeed in their challenges.

But again: The key is to understand how power works—and how bias works, so you can take effective action.[86] And if that feels complicated, think of the image of David, in his battle with Goliath, and how he took a perceived disadvantage and turned it into a strength.

## 4) Double-Down

Not all the sources of power come with such quandaries. Find one that works and then take it into a higher gear:

- A strong and dynamic network, particularly being a super connector or having other super connectors within it, grows exponentially—creating visibility, relationships and the ability to benefit from brokerage opportunities.

- A strong brand, fueled these days by social media, can grow exponentially as well. Being perceived as an ascending star, for example, can lead to all sorts of amazing things—from high profile people and publications wanting to be connected to you or feature you, to executive recruiters constantly knocking at your door, which in turn creates a virtuous cycle—and gives you power and leverage with your boss if they are not keeping you happy.

## 5) Find Strength in Numbers

Allies has become an overused term, but there is strength in numbers. Numerous studies, dating back to Rosabeth M. Kanter's pioneering work at Harvard, have shown that a critical mass is better for change, compared to one lone or token individual. Form allies because allies support you, defend you, sponsor you, and have your interests at heart.

## 6) Success and Power Attracts

People are attracted to, or at a minimum generally more tolerant of, those who are successful and powerful. People want to be associated with winners for a host of well documented psychological, material, or self-interested reasons. And because people want to be associated with power—and because of the power we gain when we hit the top—people will tend to excuse any bad behavior, or it often goes unpunished.

This is simply to say that if you grow your power, it's likely that mistakes, transgressions, even enemies you may have made along the way, will be brushed under the carpet. And that you will be able to rewrite history in ways that reinforce your desired narrative or rewrite the rules if you so choose. That's what power can bring.

I'm not going to make any moral or ethical judgments here—I leave that to you—but I offer this last point by asking: "What do you have to lose—and what do you have to gain—by taking some risk, by going for it, to build power?" It sucks to be on the bottom, and frankly, if you really want to make change, it helps immensely to have power.

## Going Forward

So, to answer Lisa's question: What's she (or someone like her) supposed to do in her presentation next week? In how she spends her time this month?

She needs to build her personal power, supercharging it by embracing the sources of power and taking into account the six considerations above—but, most importantly, as will see after this chapter, by leaping off the Rock to the Map and the Snowball, which is about putting things in action to advance.

Understand power, understand the context and bias, and take action. Use the information to inform and guide you, not stop you. The game is not fair. Don't be paralyzed. Get rid of any self-limiting behavior or mental models that hold you back. (After all, that's what those in power would like, and benefit from, from you staying in your lane).

Follow Sheryl Sandberg's advice and *Lean In*.[87] You know it won't be easy—but nothing in your life to date has been either.

Personally, I'm optimistic, having worked with so many diverse executives and how learning to build power has disproportionately helped those who are women or minorities. I have seen how power has transformed them, and increased their confidence, and opened the corridors of power to them. As Inbal Demri says, *"You need power, a seat at the table. Because if you are not at the table, you are probably on the menu. If you can't build your seat at the table, build your own table and have others work to claim a seat there."*

**Takeaways (challenges that women and other groups face):**

The world is not fair. The system, and its bias, needs to be changed, but deep structural change will not happen anytime soon. Focus on what you *can* control, which is building your personal power. Specifically: 1) Remember that the theories of power are universal, but that you may need to adjust your strategies based on context or biases. Don't throw the baby out with the bathwater! The key is understanding how power works, and how biases operate, so you pick winning strategies. 2) Apply "judo", turning weakness into strengths, if required—or simply double-down on power-building behaviors, like expanding your network and building your brand. 3) Find strength in numbers through allies that will support you. Above all, realize building power and gaining success

GET PROMOTED | 161

attracts others, even your former adversaries, and allows you to write the rules. You want a seat at the table, instead of being on the menu.

**A note to all:**

Gender, race, and power is a sensitive topic, and I hope that I have treated it successfully, and with care, in this section. These topics are often the elephant in the room, but I believe we benefit from frank conversations.

This chapter is important to everyone, not just women and people of color, for two reasons:

First, understanding the six points above will give you a nuanced view on power. I've seen all my clients benefit from expanding their playbook.

Second, understanding how others experience bias makes everyone better off. This knowledge will make you a better colleague, boss, advisor, mentor, ally, or sponsor since you'll have more empathy, or be able to offer strategies that work, that are not untethered from reality.

Finally, I want to thank all my amazing clients, especially the 70% of whom are women, minorities, immigrants or come from historically marginalized groups. The diversity of my client base has been more than an enriching experience. Although I am mixed race and have lived and worked around the globe, it is precisely because I do not share the same "lived experience," as many of my clients that I have strived to become more in tune with them—and made me spend countless hours reviewing academic studies, and evidenced-based literature, so that my recommendations would be practical yet firmly grounded in reality. And that has made me an infinitely better, and I would like to believe, more effective executive coach.

# CHAPTER 7

# How Real People Build Power at Work

You've seen the substantial evidence of what leads to success and what can make you more powerful, which will help you to ascend in your organization and be able to get more things done.

Ask yourself, again:

- What are the implications of this hard evidence for you?
- How have these points played out in your past life or organizations, for good, bad... or worse?
- And most importantly, what might you do differently to get ahead?

One of my jobs as an executive coach is to help my clients expand their perspectives and mental models, helping them realize they have greater choices at their disposal.

In this chapter, I'll make the evidence tangible by providing examples of what my clients have done to get out of their own way, learn new skills (or unlearn old ones), and build power.

They are not only inspiring, but very instructive. They show how each client applied the principles and lessons in strategic, sometimes creative, but all very intentional ways to help themselves in their own situation.

## Political Skills: Jenn's Story

**Situation:** Jenn (not her real name) joined a leading automotive parts supplier. Jenn had been working for a terrible organization and was demoralized and eventually left. She felt part of her challenge was failing to navigate the politics of dealing with tough personalities and turf wars. In her new position, where she had a senior role and reported to the CEO, she wanted to set a strong tone and manage key stakeholders early.

**What she did:** She went through some hard self-reflection, and I conducted a 360 assessment from colleagues at her previous employers, who emphasized how she had tried often to go alone, instead of working with other key stakeholders. Based on that, she spent significant time analyzing the power structure in the new company (using a tool called the Power Map, which we will see in more depth in Chapter 9). She analyzed their backgrounds and history, and from day one went on a listening tour, built relationships, and further refined her knowledge of each. By doing so, she was able to be more in tune with their agendas, hot spots, ways of working, who influenced them—as well as see which two executives really had power.

**Results:** Within three months she was the CEO's trusted right hand, had her budgets approved easily, and was able to marshal support for change initiatives. She learned to let go of some of her past behaviors which rankled people. And she became more focused—both on who mattered and what mattered, and how to get things done. Before she hit the year mark, she received an off the charts raise and bonus and is in discussion with the CEO to take on a second-in-command role.

## Networks: Alex's Story

**Situation:** Alex (not his real name) had a terrible boss who was biased against him, micromanaged, and stole all the credit. For years, Alex toiled in relative obscurity, being passed over for promotions. He was making good money but felt stalled and angry. Working harder seemed to make no difference, and fighting his boss only made things worse.

**What he did:** Alex realized his boss wasn't going to change, and if he wanted to get promoted or take on a new role, he needed to build his network and visibility, first inside the organization. Alex broke rank and found a fellow alum higher up in the organization. In a mentoring conversation with that alum, Alex presented a new breakthrough idea and asked for that executive's opinion and support. The executive supported the concept and Alex, which eventually led Alex to present the idea directly to the CEO. The CEO funded it!

This time, the boss could not steal the idea, and word of Alex's breakthrough got him noticed more broadly. Alex used his increased profile to meet the heads of other departments. That helped his team develop the new product faster and got him out from under the shadow of his domineering boss.

**Results:** Alex did not get promoted—the boss promoted a favorite. But Alex was now more widely known and able to approach key executives more freely. Alex's bonus that year was by far his largest ever. As he told me, "While I don't want to leave this group, I clearly did something right because that bonus felt great." Post-coaching, he applied the principles to create a monthly roundtable of executives across the company, inviting experts and creating mentoring partnerships across the group. That, he told me, has made networking easier for him and has created visibility and a brand as an internal innovator.

---

**1 minute exercise: the "Other" strategy:**

**Channel others to power yourself**

I see it all the time. Some executives have a hard time asking their boss for a promotion, negotiating more resources and headcount for their unit, or taking credit for their amazing work. They find doing any of these things selfish and aggressive. Because they find it uncomfortable, they end up not taking action or pulling back.

If you are a self-effacing giver that has a hard time asserting for yourself, here's a simple strategy that can help:

Ask yourself who else, besides you, will benefit if you get the promotion, get more resources, or get credit.

**What you might say:**

A better network and resources will benefit my hard-working team, who always does more with less.

A promotion will inspire my kids and other people like me in the company, who see me as a role model.

A raise will benefit my family, who has long supported me.

More resources will help me finally launch that product, which will benefit customers or extend our company mission.

Credit and recognition will get me a seat on an important committee that is shaping company policy, which will benefit everyone.

When you see things this way, helping yourself is actually about helping *other people*. And for many executives—particularly women—seeing things as being more about others, and less about them, greatly increases their conviction, assertiveness, and ability to take action—and get what they want.

So, when you find yourself pulling back because you feel it's all about you, think again: Who else will benefit?

Channel others to power yourself.

## Visibility and Brand—Victoria's Story

**Situation:** Victoria (not her real name) was a head-down top performer, young, and ambitious. Colleagues were jealous; top executives felt she should put in more time and rotate around to lateral roles before being promoted to senior director. Victoria recognized she needed to learn but felt like she would stagnate if she had to rotate around.

**What she did:** Rather than "stay in her lane," Victoria actively sought out top executives for advice. She converted those relationships into mentorships and sponsorships. She sought out any executives, women and men, whom she believed had expertise, skills, or influence that she could learn or benefit from.

At the same time, she started a blog on LinkedIn, writing about insights in her field. As a relatively young woman of color, she stood out among her peers. That got her noticed and attracted a large following, which then led to an interview in the press. Then she got noticed and was featured in a top 30 list in a magazine.

**Results:** Those strategic steps built her brand and got her noticed. She got promoted to senior director in record time.

Recruiters were increasingly approaching her as well, making her keenly aware of her market value.

## Executive Presence and Communication—Chen's Story

**Situation:** Chen (not his real name) was a stellar performer, stalled at director in his biotech's division. He wanted to rise but was being passed over, partly because his group had a smaller scope. A new lateral role gave him an opportunity, and he wanted to nail it and use it to get an overdue promotion.

**What he did:** When I conducted a 360, senior management said Chen was "not showing up like a leader." When pressed for details, they said he ran projects well but showed up like he was "reporting the news" rather than "delivering strong recommendations." He had these powerful ideas but would present and act in ways ("I think," "maybe") that unwittingly undercut his perception and brand. He removed limiting language, we recorded him practicing—and he felt empowered to take strong stands on issues.

**Results:** Chen not only started to notice senior executives react to him differently, but he also started to feel more confident. His boss became his advocate, and his leadership ratings rose. He got promoted in the next cycle and has interesting offers in other divisions as well.

All of these executives were stalled or not sure what to do. They saw what they were really missing at work, got out of their own way, and started doing the right activities to advance their careers.

Now let's turn to The Map—your strategic view of the organization and your goals.

**Manage your career like a top sales rep?!**

"What?" many of my clients ask me in disbelief and disgust. "You want me to learn from *salespeople*?"

That's right. If you agree that political skills and influence are the keys to rising in your career, then you need to study the masters of influence.

Most people, however, see sales reps as sleazy, undereducated, "coin-operated" hacks. Sales doesn't have the cache of its sexier peer, marketing. It's not even taught in most MBA programs. So, sales gets dismissed.

That's a shame because there is so much to learn from them.

Here are five habits of top sales reps (note I say *top* sales reps, not average ones) that can help you accelerate your career:

1) **Advance other people's interests to advance your own:** It's not what you sell, it's what they buy, so you need to know what other people want. Approach colleagues like customers.

2) **Map where the power lies:** B2B reps sell into complex environments. They need to identify the decision maker, influencers, blockers, or they waste a lot of time (and money—the cost of a top field sales can exceed thousands of dollars a day). Have you looked at how you spend your valuable time? You should make a map too (we'll do that in Part II when you create your Power Map).

3) **Get noticed and engaged:** You not only need to identify the right people, but you need to get their attention. Reps need to get in but eventually close the sale. They learn all the techniques. With information overload these days, selling insights to open the door is critical.

4) **Understand the network:** Information, access and visibility with the right people is critical, so reps take actions or positions (like embed themselves in a process) that are strategic. They want to identify needs where their solutions fit or where they can add value.

5) **They do and are persistent:** Marketers can pontificate and share fancy buzzwords, but salespeople need to close. They must get used to people saying no, which they reframe as learning.

Dan Pink started to make selling a bit more accepted in his bestseller *To Sell Is Human*. He calls the new ABC of selling as "Attunement, Buoyancy and Clarity." Ring familiar?

As the late Rodney Dangerfield said, "I don't get no respect." It's high time sales reps get theirs.[88]

# CHAPTER 8

# Results Today: An Experiment (Do This Now)

*"We hold ourselves back in ways both big and small,
by lacking self-confidence, by not raising our hands,
and by pulling back when we should be leaning in."*
- Sheryl Sandberg

I lied that we would proceed to Part II, the Map.

From having worked with countless executives around the globe, I know that most people about now—maybe you—start to grow tired of the argument, even though we've seen the evidence and you've seen people like you put that into action to become more successful.

You "agree" at an intellectual level but not an emotional one, which makes you reluctant to take action. That's understandable. It is not easy to leap off The Rock. You're jumping into unfamiliar and uncomfortable territory.

Coaches help you test assumptions or identify small experiments to help you advance.

So, before we proceed further, I want you to conduct an experiment… one that will likely give you some results as soon as today. I promise it will be simple, and I promise you'll learn something valuable from the 20 minutes you'll invest.

Follow the steps and worksheet on the following pages and make sure to go do it (yes, go out and do it), then come back and reflect.

Only then read on. That's when I will share what the experiment reveals, and why it holds the key to success with The Map and The Snowball.

## The Experiment (Instructions)

In this experiment you will ask for something.

This is what I want you to do:

Ask for something, something you want or need but feel a bit awkward asking for.

Ideally, it is something at work.

You could ask for:

- Someone to do something for you
- Additional resources for a project
- A meeting with a key person
- A raise

Sure, this may feel a bit uncomfortable. That's why you're reading this book. It's time to get out of your comfort zone and break out of your normal routine and way of doing things.

Fill out the worksheet on the following page.

# Experiment Worksheet

DATE: _____

MY ASK: _____

WHY I AM ASKING FOR IT (REASON): _____

% PROBABILITY I WILL GET WHAT I ASK FOR (0-100%)_____

Before proceeding, go back to what you wrote above and be bolder.

Be more ambitious and ask for more than you normally would.

I'd encourage you to make more than one ask. Additional "asks" could be at home. You could ask for a discount at a store. Or a friend or family member to do something for you. Or a stranger to lend you their cell phone or some money.

In fact, the more of these "asks" you do this week, the better. If you want to record them, you can do so here:

DATE: _____

MY ASK: _____

WHY I AM ASKING FOR IT (REASON): _____

% PROBABILITY I WILL GET WHAT I ASK FOR (0-100%)_____


DATE: _____

MY ASK: _____

WHY I AM ASKING FOR IT (REASON): _____

% PROBABILITY I WILL GET WHAT I ASK FOR (0-100%)_____

Now, go make your asks. After you have done them, debrief what happened on the next page.

## Experiment Debrief

Report and reflect on what happened, here, answering the following questions:

- What did you do?
- How did you feel doing it?
- What happened?
- What worked?
- What didn't work?
- Anything surprising happen?
- Any learning?
- How would you use this in a different situation?
- How might you change your ask to get more of what you want?

**Move on only after you have finished doing and writing down your reflection.**

## Experiment Debrief: The Power of Asking

*"Now, I've actually always found something to be
very true, which is most people don't get those
experiences because they never ask. I've never found
anybody who didn't want to help me when
I've asked them for help."*
- Steve Jobs

How did asking work out?

I bet it felt a bit uncomfortable. Most of us are reluctant to ask. If it didn't feel uncomfortable, you probably weren't ambitious and bold enough.

Did you get what you asked for?

The simple fact is that most people don't get anything—because they don't even ask.

For those who do ask, the evidence would say you were up to 50% more likely to get what you asked for than you had expected. That's right: a whopping 50%.[89] It does appear the adage is true: "Ask and ye shall receive." We dramatically underestimate how likely others are to help us, according to researchers at Stanford who ran the studies.

What insights did your experiment generate?

If you got what you wanted, how do you feel now? Probably emboldened to do it again: It worked!

If you did not, take heart: You probably learned what doesn't work, which is valuable too.

How might you enhance the probability people will say yes to a request?

In one study conducted at Harvard, people used different wording to ask if they could cut ahead in a photocopier line.[90]

- One ask: "Excuse me, I have 5 pages. May I use the Xerox machine?"
- The other ask: "Excuse me, I have 5 pages. May I use the Xerox machine because I have to make copies?"
- Yet another ask: "Excuse me, I have 5 pages. May I use the Xerox machine because I'm in a rush?"

The first request got 60% compliance. The third got 94% compliance. And the second got 93% compliance.

That's right: just adding the word "because"—and stating a reason, even one that is not compelling ("because I have to make copies") dramatically increased compliance.

Additionally, the researchers who calculated how off our estimates can be suggest that we should pay more attention to how our request is being made, compared to the size of our request.

Research on persuasion, negotiation strategies, and coalition building give us even more insight into other critical factors that increase the likelihood others will comply, or say yes:[91]

- The way we sequence requests, or anchor people
- The way we frame information (where we focus the spotlight, from whose point of view we present that information)
- The way we get others to like us or see us as credible
- How we present, for example in person or via other mediums

Of course, experiments don't always work (which is why they are called experiments).

But, given what we know about the research, asking will work more often than you think it will. And when you find out what doesn't work, you can then narrow down or get to an approach that might.

What does this have to do with building power and getting ahead?

Well, powerful people ask for things, and most people want to help us. When you even feel powerful, you tend to ask for things more assertively or more convincingly.

You might think of asking as being demanding… or being aggressive. So, you don't ask.

Don't overlook a very simple way to build power: Ask. Your team is looking to you to ask (or tell) them to do things. They also depend on you asking for a budget to ensure they have the resources to do their job.

Remember, at this point, this is just a simple experiment that shows the power of experimenting, or taking action, to create new insight and accelerate your mindset shift.

**Ask for advice:**

When people feel good about themselves, they are predisposed to the source or messenger. And there is no better way to warm up a relationship than to flatter someone.

Yet most clients I work with are reluctant to flatter. They find it fake, or that it won't work where they come from.

So, consider asking for advice—instead of asking for feedback. Feedback can often come across as someone pointing out your weaknesses.

Seeking advice is a form of flattery because you're saying someone knows more than you, you value them. It also creates a bond, like a partnership. When you ask for advice, you appeal to a person's pride and vanity, you give them a chance to display their knowledge... and they will admire your good judgment in coming to them for help.

If that still feels awkward, be sincere. Everyone—even your adversaries—have something good about them. Sincerely ask for advice. Not only will you gain new insight, but you may also start building an important relationship in your organization.[92]

## Experiment: Real Examples

> *"You miss 100 percent of the shots you do not take."*
> *- Michael Jordan*

Now, I want to share what a few of my clients experienced when they did this exercise.

### Getting a Raise

A client I started working with was frustrated: He was passed over for promotions and didn't receive the raise or bonus he expected. He felt his performance was strong but was upset the boss did not see it.

"Have you asked him or presented your case?" I asked.

He provided every reason why he had not: The moment wasn't right, it would be awkward, it would be aggressive, the boss would say no.

"What do you have to lose? What's the worst that can happen?" I said.

He agreed there was little risk, except his ego taking a hit if he got rejected.

I got a text message the next day:

> *"My boss agreed to give me a larger bonus on the spot. He was also open to a promotion discussion, which has now been scheduled."*

Keep in mind the goal of our coaching was to increase his compensation and a promotion, and he landed most of that after our first session.

## Asking for (and Getting) Resources

A young executive was a killer performer and was bringing in results with half the headcount of one of her peers. She felt overworked but always liked to prove she could do more with less.

But it was tiring. She was puzzled that her peers always clocked out at 6 p.m. on the dot, got the same or worse results... and yet the boss and her boss seemed happy.

"So, how could you get more resources, more headcount?" I asked.

She said there was no budget, and it was early in the relationship working for that boss, and she first needed to prove herself. Meanwhile she was close to burnout, and so was her team, trying to "prove themselves" over and over.

We worked on "ask" strategies, and she did.

In the next session she said she not only got two new people added to her team, but the boss heard her ambition and promised to budget in resources for her to launch into a new market in the upcoming year.

## Mentored by a Senior Leader

A high-level executive was getting passed over for promotions and top assignments, and when we talked about it, he realized that others seemed to have sponsors in the C-Suite and at the board level.

"What could a mentor or sponsor do for you?" I asked.

He felt they could do a lot but then rattled off why it had not occurred: They should come to me, they should see my talent and potential, it would be awkward if I ask and they say no… what if it doesn't work out.

"What could you do about that?" I replied.

He identified three top executives, potential mentors, and asked for a 1-1 meeting to get their career advice.

One never responded, but the other two said yes immediately.

In the meetings, there wasn't good chemistry with one, but he hit it off with the other. He asked if they could do monthly mentoring sessions and that senior leader agreed. They are now meeting every month.

To think the executive had been waiting a year for a mentor to come to him!

Three months later, the one senior executive (the one he didn't have chemistry with), proactively pointed out an interesting project.

And through the ongoing mentoring with the other executive, my client got strong feedback on how he was showing up, what he needed to do if he wanted to rise—and improved it. Five months later, that mentor provided my client with a tip that the company planned to open a new division in the next reorg and suggested my client should apply early—and the mentor would be happy to put a word in with the hiring VP. Doors opened.

## Win or Learn

Does asking always work as well as it did in these examples?

Of course not.

Remember: You miss 100% of the shots you do not take.

The upside of asking comes in two ways:

First, if you succeed or get a yes, you get instant results that move you forward.

Second, even if you get a no, you get new information, which often produces new insight. (And you also might not waste countless hours planning or fretting at night about something that might never happen).

For the executive who sought a sponsor, two of his three "asks" technically failed. But from those two he learned what approaches did not work—and he got used to stepping up and asking.

Persistence in asking pays, and every "failure" is not really failure, particularly if you seek feedback and learn from it. As Thomas Edison said, "I have not failed. I've just found 10,000 ways that won't work."

## Action Drives Insight

The takeaway here is that action drives insight, not the other way around. Which is why I wanted you to do this exercise.

The other reason why this exercise is important can be found in the work of Swedish psychologist, K. Anders Ericsson, who popularized the idea of deliberate practice. Ericsson studied top performers in music, sports, software design, and other fields. What he found was that no matter what they were doing, the best of the best improved their abilities in very similar ways.

He called this principle deliberate practice. It stresses that talent is not enough, that we need to practice and take focused, repeated actions—breaking things down into manageable parts and incorporating feedback along the way.

In these examples, the clients took action and practiced their asks, getting feedback from me and others.

As you build power to grow your career, think about how action drives insights and how deliberate practice is the key to improvement.

So, as we look back at the sources of power, and we move forward into strategic and tactical actions, think about what you can begin to experiment with, and how you will practice it. That will unleash you, freeing you from those myths holding you back.

**Is this all about being uncomfortable?**

Learning new things often is uncomfortable, even if that is where we grow and learn the most.

Think about when you first learned to ride a bike or swim or had to take your performance in either of those areas to a new level, as if you were preparing for your first triathlon. Think of that as a metaphor for learning the important political skills that will propel you. In the working world, as you rise beyond individual contributor to manager and leader, you are no longer doing 5K runs. You are now doing triathlons, moving through more varied territory, where you need a wider skillset. Entering those triathlons aren't your average people—they are other seasoned athletes looking for every edge themselves to succeed.

Under what logic is doing more walking going to help you? Embrace new areas to grow.

# PART II
# The Map

"A compass, I learnt when I was surveying, it'll point you True North from where you are standing, but it's got no advice about the swamps and deserts and chasms you'll encounter along the way. If in pursuit of your destination, you plunge ahead, heedless of obstacles, and achieve nothing more than to sink in a swamp, what's the use of knowing True North?"

– Abraham Lincoln in the Steven Spielberg film *Lincoln*.

## Summary

You're now starting to Get Real, having been exposed to The Rock (the hard truth) and, by looking at yourself and your organization, you see that you may have believed in the myths about what it takes to rise through the ranks....

Then you did a small experiment. You did what powerful, successful people do, something you may have shied away from in the past because it was uncomfortable.

That act of asking may have gotten you something you wanted. Or maybe it didn't exactly work, but the act of doing it revealed new insights. Action led to insight, and deliberate practice will help you build that muscle.

Before you plunge forward with all your newfound realizations, it's important to Get Strategic. You need to know where to start, what path you should take, and where your odds are greatest for success. You need to see the landscape.

For that, you need The Map.

That Map was sitting in front of you all along—you just didn't know how to read it.

That's what we tackle next.

# CHAPTER 9

# The Power Map

If you want to get somewhere, it helps to have a map.

- What is your destination, or goal?
- What are the paths to get there?
- What obstacles are out there to be aware of?
- Is there a shortcut or easier way?
- What might help you get there faster?
- What might you be missing, that you don't even see?

You not only want a map, but you want the one that is most up to date.

Even better, you'd love a fancy smart map, like you get with an app like Waze, that will tell you about accidents ahead of time, which hours have the most traffic—and the best ways to reroute if you need to.

To get promoted and move the needle at work, wouldn't it be great to have a Waze, helping you navigate your organization?

But is there such a map?

Yes—but most people don't bother to look for it. And those that do, usually look in the wrong places for it.

You need the Power Map.

The Power Map has been one of the most successful tools in my coaching practice, which I developed years ago and have honed working with clients, observing what most helped them unlock insights that propelled their ascent.

As Lincoln said, knowing your destination is useless unless you know how to navigate the terrain to get there.

## What the Power Map Can Uncover

The Power Map is an effective goal-achieving tool, whether you are:

- Seeking a promotion or role change
- Managing a work transition
- Entering a new job
- Executing an important initiative
- Trying to implement change, and face resistance

It gives you the "lay of the land," helping you determine:

- Who is critical on your path to success
- Why those on your critical path are important, and what they care about
- Paths and strategies that will most help you influence and advance

- Paths and strategies that won't help you or will set you back

Your Power Map will open your eyes to what I call "influence assets". These are the opportunities for influence you already have (and probably aren't using) and illuminate new paths of influence that you need to create (which are simpler than you think).

Your Power Map will also show you what I call "influence conduits." These are areas where you should channel your time and energy, and help you determine the best strategy to pursue.

Let me emphasize straight away that the Power Map is not the organizational chart or a stakeholder inventory. There may be some overlap, but the Power Map is different in one critical way: Instead of looking at the people through their title, it focuses on who holds power, and why.

**The Power Map (Summary)**

You can download a copy of my 1-page Power Map tool, here: (https://changwenderoth.com/the-power-map/)

It covers 3 Steps:

1. Your Goal
2. Mapping Key Individuals in the Landscape
   a. Business Needs
   b. Personal Needs

    c.   Background

    d.   Sources of Power

    e.   Hot Buttons

    f.   Who influences them/connections

    g.   Your relationship with them

    h.   What you don't know

3.   Your Next Steps (Who-How-When)

## The Power Map in Action (An Example)

To understand the Power Map, let's walk through a real example of my client, Marta (not her real name):

- **Her situation:** Marta was a talented, high performer responsible for growing sales and key clients for a global company in an emerging market.

- **Her goal:** She wanted to get promoted, to lead all commercial business in her region—and eventually to join global headquarters in a broader, strategic role. She wanted to see the world, learn and work with the best talent in headquarters, and bring her insights and experience in her emerging market to help the business. She was great at identifying and implementing innovative, new go-to-market models in her territory and had been recognized repeatedly with top sales awards for it.

- **Her challenge:** For three straight years she had exceeded her sales and performance targets. The best practices she had created and implemented had been heralded and embraced by other territories. But when a regional leadership role opened up—leading sales, marketing, and distribution strategy across her entire region—she was passed over. A less dynamic peer, who had stature and tenure but produced average results, got the job. She was frustrated. It was clear that continuing to work hard and produce fantastic results was not going to get her promoted. But she was unsure where to start and what she should be doing differently.

To gain a fresh perspective, Marta created her Power Map:

1. **She clarified her goal: What did she really want and why?**

   She wanted to rise to a regional leadership role or even better into global headquarters, where she could make a larger impact.

   She wanted to shape company strategy, not just execute. A promotion would be recognition and reward of her great work, smarts, and help her feel that she was growing personally and professionally. The regional role might not result in a huge bump in salary, but a job in headquarters could double her salary.

   Writing down her goal in one sentence really got Marta to focus and not avoid what she really wanted.

   So, make sure to write down your goal. It can be scary but also liberating. Too many people dance around what they really want, usually out of fear they will fail or will be laughed at. If your goal is vague, like "to improve my relationships," ask yourself what will happen if you improve your relationships? That can help you get at the big ambitious goal you deserve and are probably shying away from.

2. **She identified the individuals that had the most power to make her goal happen: Who had the most power? In other words, who would have the biggest say in the decision, by virtue of their authority, budget, resources, influence?**

To get promoted within her region, into the leadership circle, the regional president had final say, and often the biggest voice. After all, he had nominated and promoted the less dynamic peer instead of her.

But to get promoted in headquarters, the regional president did not make the call. There, the worldwide SVP of International had built the team she wanted to be part of. The SVP also approved new global initiatives and approved budget and headcount.

Remember that organizations are made of people, and people make decisions. As Dan Sullivan, CEO of Strategic Coach, reminds us, first ask: "Who not how."

**2a-2d:** For each individual, she then listed their needs, backgrounds, and sources of power:

Marta had been in the company six years, so had a good sense of the answers:

- **2a: Their "business needs"** - Business needs include goals, key priorities, pain points.

  Both had sales targets, focused on revenue, and managed a P&L, which was the clear driver of their compensation.

  The regional president, however, seemed to care most about one key account which drove 30% of the region's revenue.

  The SVP of International seemed increasingly focused this year on growing a new product line. He had emphasized it repeatedly in presentations and recently put one of his top direct reports to oversee it.

- **2b: Their "personal needs"** - Personal needs are more about people's identities, what feeds their egos.

  Like most people, both executives liked praise from their bosses.

  The regional president, however, loved being highlighted in the local media, and he tweeted often about a charity group. He also seemed comfortable in his role and did not seem ambitious about being promoted.

  The SVP of International, now in his early 60s, spoke a lot about "impact." He seemed intent on the legacy he would leave, and some said he was carving out a path to retirement or landing future consulting or board roles.

- **2c: Their backgrounds** - Where did these people work in the past, go to school and study, do for fun?

    The regional president worked his way up through sales and mixed socially with customers and industry heads in the region, playing golf with many at his country club.

    The SVP of International was an engineer, product of elite western schools. He had spent decades with a well-known multinational before joining this firm; in fact many of his direct reports he had brought over with him. He was an avid photographer and runner, who loved to travel.

- **2d: Their sources of power** - Why do people listen or follow them? Recall the sources of power in Chapter 5. Remember the definition of power (controlling resources that others value), and how power falls into two groups: hard and soft. Look specifically at their network, visibility and brand, and their presence and communication skills.

    The regional president had hard power: He controlled budgets, new hires, promotions, and final end-of-year bonuses. There was a committee, but he signed off and often got involved in decisions. While he listened or sought the opinion of his leadership team, it was clear he used this power to reward or punish. He also had soft power that people valued, through his network and relationships: He knew all the key clients and regulators in the region, enabling him to help close big deals. He also had a direct line to the global CEO, given they worked together earlier in their career at a previous company. Finally, he was charismatic: When he spoke, customers and employees felt proud of the company.

The SVP of International also had hard power as he managed the strategy and P&L of the fastest growing revenue source in the company, and the global CEO gave him free rein. But a big source of his power came from two of his direct reports, ones who had worked for him for years at this company and previous ones. He trusted them entirely, and he always seemed to turn to them to execute projects and update him as he "didn't get into the weeds". He also had a strong reputation: He had an impressive track record of innovation, which people talked about in the company, and got him company and industry awards.

## Focus on Self-Interest and Identity

Identifying the top 1-2 individuals felt restrictive, but it really got Marta to focus and examine small but important details of what made these two so important in the organization.

To diagnose the landscape well, you need to look beyond the 2-dimensional organization chart of names and titles.

Most importantly, she dug into the two most critical areas: their self-interest and their identity.

Self-interest is critical because it's basic human behavior that we act in ways that benefit us or protect and preserve those close to us. If you can help someone get more of what they want or need, you are likely to be seen as valuable. Self-interest could be material but could also be related to one's ego.

Identity is critical because we want to feel good about ourselves: how we are known, how we define ourselves.

If you can tap into either of these sources, your influence—and your ability to build power—will skyrocket.

**Be a detective**

So, how do you find all this information?

Unfortunately, you can't download an app and get all this information instantly. People don't typically advertise their motivations and needs on their foreheads.

To uncover this information, you need to be a good observer, and you need to ask good questions.

**A starter checklist:**

**Look up their profiles.** There are a lot of free tools at your disposal. First, do a Google search, check LinkedIn, Twitter, Facebook, and particularly see what they like or comment about online.

**Observe them.** Pay attention to what they say (or even more important don't say), who they spend their time with, how they behave around others. You can learn a lot if you simply observe a meeting and see how they interact. Who do they pay attention or respect to, when do they ignore a person and start reading their cell phone?

**Ask others who know them well.** Get insight from people who know them well. Often these people are in unexpected places. An executive assistant or colleague who worked with them at a former company can shed light on how the person makes decisions, pet peeves, and personal habits. A person with insight might even be *outside the organization*, like the external consultant they hire for every project. And people who work across the organization, like project managers or leaders who have made many lateral moves, can have a wide perspective. Good questions will take you far: "So, what seems to be the top focus for him/her now?" "How do people best approach him/her with a new idea?"

**Ask them directly.** Sometimes the easiest path is to just ask. Good questions that get beneath the surface to get at their true motivations: "What do you want you to achieve by year-end?" "What will make us as a team most successful?" "What aspect of the business most keeps you awake at night?" "Who do you advise me to speak to; who can provide the most insight?"

Start simple and approach the task like a detective. Observe carefully, ask good questions, and seek out multiple sources to corroborate what you learn.

If you have been in an organization for a while, you should have a good sense of these things. If you don't, you better start! If you are new to an organization, all the more reason to build the map—even if it helps you realize what you don't know.

In fact, creating a strong Power map can itself be a source of power: You see how to navigate around, connect, and broker valuable information to others. Information is power.

Marta then continued to round out her map:

- **2e-f: For each individual, what are their hot buttons and who influences them**: What rubs them the wrong way (land mines to avoid), and who else do they listen or defer to (influence conduits)?

- **2e: Their hot buttons:** An executive assistant said that the regional president had to receive reports using a particular template, or he would dismiss the message. Her direct boss, who had interacted with the SVP of

International more than her, shared over lunch that the SVP detested a new Marketing VP in headquarters because the VP was more into "branding" image than driving sales results.

- **2f: Who influences them:** The regional president had a leadership team but relied on the finance director's opinion the most because he gave him updated figures and managed the money. Curiously, he liked two older field sales reps, way down in the organization. One person said he used them as his "ears on the ground." The executive assistant also seemed to have his ear as he managed the schedule and media appearances.

  The SVP of International had those two direct reports he trusted entirely. Recently, he had promoted one employee from European sales on his team. And then there was the outside consultant, who he kept hiring for strategy projects.

Understanding the web of relationships helped complete the picture: who was important, what they valued, how they derived their power, who influenced them.

> **Repeat 2a-f: Go deeper on the new individuals that emcrged**: If someone is vital, dig into more information about them, to fill out the map.

> For Marta, the SVP's two direct reports warranted a closer look. They clearly valued business building ideas and helping the SVP. The promotion of the other

employee in headquarters was important because it revealed that expertise in analytics was valued.

- **2g: Rate each individual's level of influence, your relationship with each, and highlight any unknowns:** Who really has the most influence? Are they favorable to you? Neutral? Opposed? (Or perhaps don't know you at all?)

The regional president was neutral to her: He was happy she produced great results but had his close group already on the leadership team. The two salespeople didn't like her at all.

The SVP of International had signed off on sponsoring her for an executive education program, and he had also sent a congratulatory email to her and her boss when she got a sales award, but she couldn't be sure if he really knew her. She didn't know the direct reports at all.

- **2h: What she didn't know:** There's no way you can uncover everything. And organizations change, so you need to update your Map periodically.

Marta did not know much about the SVP's two key direct reports. They didn't have public profiles, and she had never met them. She needed to know more.

# Unexpected Insights, That Reveal the Way Forward

You might feel a bit exhausted going through Marta's process, but you needed to see how it really works.

And the Power Map is actually faster to create—and more important—than most clients believe.

Marta's Power Map is captured on one page. She did her first pass in less than an hour then gathered more info over the week through 1-1 meetings and casual conversations.

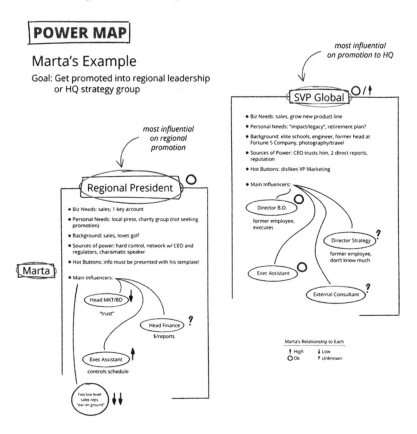

Marta worked in B2B sales, and after making her map, she realized she had not taken the same discipline she did with complex accounts to map out her own organization, to chart her own career.

Insights that emerged for Marta, and countless executives have shared with me as well:

- **The Power Map doesn't look like the Org chart.**
  The Power Map revealed the *informal*—and more important—network. Power tends to sit upward in an organization (sorry, despite all the hype, organizations today are still not that flat), but titles, positions, and authority aren't always the best indicator of influence.

  Compare Marta's Power Map to the organization chart (page 209). Marta's boss who reported to the regional president was notably absent on the Power Map. He was a great guy but not really that important or influential. The executive assistant was more useful. The two direct reports of the SVP of International didn't have fancy titles but had the regional president's inner ear.

- **What is important to people is not always obvious. Personal needs (ego) tend to be even more important the higher you go.**
  The SVP of International cared about hitting sales targets, but it was clear that one particular initiative was getting his attention—selling one product that corporate had just launched. He also was close to

retirement, so planning his next step and leaving a legacy mattered, probably more than another six figures in his pocket (his annual compensation was already seven figures).

In her region, the president had a comfortable and secure perch. It was pretty clear, the more Marta studied it, that he really loved being featured in the media and speaking in front of audiences because it enhanced his reputation in his community. The executive assistant confided that the president would clear his schedule to speak to journalists.

- **Calling out what you *don't* know**
  Marta prided herself on knowing the key people in her customer accounts. So, it bugged her that she had overlooked the key people who could promote her to headquarters, those two reports. She needed to find out what made them tick and how to connect.

- **Realizing you are not spending time with the people who have influence**
  Like many people I work with, we quickly find that they are heads down with their teams, executing, supporting—assuming their results will speak for themselves. That was definitely Marta's realization. It meant she wasn't in conversation with critical people on her Power Map, which would reveal which way the strategic winds were blowing, concerns, and pains being felt by those in power – or more intelligence on how she could obtain more resources.

It's likely that someone else is doing this work and helping themselves—quite possibly at your expense. In Marta's case, the new head in the region had been taking credit for her ideas and influencing the regional president. In fact, that is what got him promoted.

By not being more political, Marta had done herself a huge disservice. Sad but true.

- **Noticing that opportunities to influence and advance have always been there.**
  She now saw what was important to the SVP of International and multiple ways she could become visible and provide value. She barely knew the two direct reports, or the newly promoted person, but it was likely they would value her technical background and would find her innovative distributor network intriguing.

In summary, the Power Map showed her the landscape and the critical path. She just needed to be more strategic and deliberate about how she spent her time.

Recall how Ferris and Templar showed that those with strong political skills rise faster? The Power Map is the tool that makes it easier to deploy those skills.

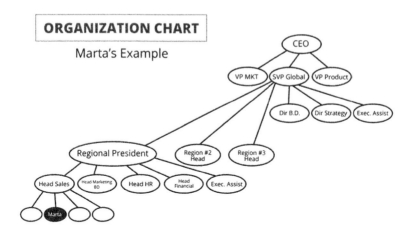

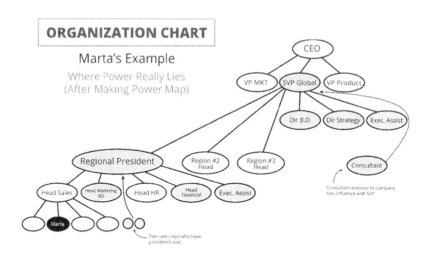

To conclude, the Power Map helps you:

- See the landscape with fresh eyes
- Discover insights into who is important and what they value
- Uncover people with influence in unsuspecting places

- Become aware of dead-ends, opposition—or people that may not be that important to your goal
- Identify "influence conduits"—how you might build relationships with people, directly, or through others. Even if you are 2-3 people removed from the power center, you can still identify an important chain of connection.
- Identify "influence assets"—the things you possess or can create that can build your power.

The Power Map gives you a huge strategic advantage and shows the way forward. No more wasted time and effort on things that won't move the needle. Marta already had a strong sense of where she had the best chance to get noticed, bring value, introduce new initiatives and ultimately get promoted.

What Marta did—the specific tactics you take to make your goal happen—we will look at more depth in Part III, the Snowball. But before she dove into taking action, she took two quick steps to better assess her odds of success, to which we turn next.

I encourage you to download the Power Map, at https://changwenderoth.com/the-power-map/, and create your own.

## The Power Map in Action

The Power Map is a versatile tool to help you navigate your organization. Examples of how it served other clients, with different goals:

## Lateral move: Alicia

**Situation:** Alicia was tired of her M&A role in an Australian conglomerate and wanted to join an emerging digital transformation group. Waiting for positions to be internally advertised would be too late.

**Power Map insight:** Her map helped her identify an overlooked "influence conduit." She discovered that a VP she knew well had previously been the boss of the new digital group head, and that VP could provide her insights—and a positive introduction. The VP pointed out that Alicia was overlooking an "influence asset"—her cross functional experience and relationships, which she developed from her M&A integration work, which the new transformation group would need badly.

## Launching a new innovative initiative: Victor

**Situation:** Victor saw a huge opportunity to transform the supply chain of his snack food maker but got resistance from his regional bosses, who only cared about sales growth and hitting their KPIs. They dismissed his efforts.

**Power Map insight:** His map helped him identify who in the company's leadership team had the clout—but also interest—in his idea. He found ways to strategically "bump" into one key executive at corporate headquarters to present the idea and had done enough research about the executive's background to make a solid first impression. He also realized two stakeholders and the CEO were influenced by any ideas coming from one prestigious school, which led him to highlight an article to favorably reshape some of the metrics by which the project and his regional bosses would be judged.

## Starting a new role on the right foot: Sandra

**Situation:** Sandra was excited to take over the Country Manager role in Canada for an investor network. She had a global boss in headquarters, but each country had an in-country board of advisors, which she was concerned about because her predecessor had clashed with two of the advisors and subsequently been let go.

**Power Map insight:** Sandra mapped out the board, drawing on insights from one long-term employee, her boss, and additional research. Even before she started, she made efforts to meet the key board members 1-1, understanding their concerns and goals. Then she strategically used social media to help amplify the bold changes the organization was going to make with her at the helm. That rallied employees, her boss and particularly the board.

## Surviving a reorganization: Daniel

**Situation:** Daniel worked for a global biotech, which seemed to reorg every six months. A new GM overseeing his team was hired. Being remote, Daniel figured it was likely he would be chopped.

**Power Map insight:** By creating a Power Map, which involved understanding the newly named GM's background and history, he honed in that her focus was on the analytics side of the business. He realized he was buried in a group of long-time employees that, while they were in charge of digital and analytical innovation, largely just project managed old ideas. He found ways to quickly differentiate himself, highlighting that he had previously worked at a leading analytics firm.

## Bringing more resources to his team and getting promoted: Nevin

**Situation:** Nevin was a senior director at a leading retail company. He was annoyed that he had the lowest title in the leadership team, and got upset when the company hired a new IT peer of his—and gave the newcomer a VP title. Nevin disliked politics and was considering leaving to do a start-up.

**Power Map insight:** His Map showed who really influenced his boss, the president, and the back channels many of them used to influence him. He saw a key influencer, the VP of sales, was on track to miss his annual targets. Nevin volunteered to co-travel with one of the field reps and the VP to help with a key account that was in jeopardy. He not only was helpful, but he got to spend the day together—lots of windshield time and meals. In that meeting, he suggested a new product opportunity, which made the VP's eyes light up. They became best buddies, and Nevin also asked for the VP to put in a word with the president. Within two weeks, Nevin had a new 4-million-dollar budget and was told he would be promoted in the next cycle.

### Don't be a deer in the headlights: lessons from Steve

Many of us have blocking bosses, making it critical we build power: network, gain visibility.

But be careful of becoming the deer in the headlights.

One of my clients, Steve, got called in for a 1-1 with his micromanaging boss.

He told my client: "I heard you were talking to Zoe (a rival, senior SVP) and talking about career opportunities? What's up with that? Not happy here?" The boss was clearly pissed, and Steve knew he would retaliate.

Luckily, he and I had role-played this scenario the week before, anticipating it might happen.

You need to prepare because otherwise you look like a deer in the headlights, a kid with his hand in the cookie jar. Failing to respond skillfully can make the situation worse and lead to retaliation.

Strategies Steve used to avoid being a deer in the headlight:

**Practice or rehearse beforehand:** If you fumble, you look guilty, and as we remember, perception is everything.

**Turn their own words back on them:** Steve's boss had told him to "get resources for the team", so that's what Steve said: "I was doing what we talked about—getting us resources."

**Refocus attention:** Steve always made sure his networking conversations were first about the business. At the end he would weave in personal discussions. So, it was easy for Steve to say, "I was in there to shore up issues on the operational front. She actually brought up some questions about career direction at the end." Sometimes you can also diffuse with humor: "I'm, of course, always looking out at my career—I get recruiters contacting me all the time."

**Network first with those you trust and keep it discrete:** Steve had been networking for months because he first focused on people he knew would be discrete. He also never put anything in email that could be forwarded around.

**Get others to come to you:** Building power will often bring people to you. So, Steve could say in many cases, "They approached me."

Mainly, Steve practiced and prepared a response. It was a bit of acting, but as we know, acting is part of your job.

# CHAPTER 10

# Study Success

Years back, a former boss gave me some of the best advice ever: When you join a new company, look for who is most successful. And then go study and figure out what the heck they are doing.

Years later, Malcom Gladwell wrote the bestseller *Outliers.* He studied what the highest performers do differently, and what we could learn from them—and apply from them to make ourselves successful.

"Study success" is the next step after your Power Map.

Depending on your goal, you may study:

- Who has been promoted
- The most successful initiatives
- Those that did better after reorgs

Remember, when you do this exercise, you may not like what you see. Think of "success" as what has worked or succeeded *in your organization*. The people who got promoted might not be your cup of tea, but they were "successful" at getting promoted.

Be non-judgmental and think about what you might be able to learn.

## The Important Revelation

Why is this exercise important?

Because it tells you one incredibly important thing: *What your organization values, what it promotes.*

As we have seen, people and leaders say one thing about what gets you promoted, but that usually doesn't match reality. You are better off knowing what is valued, or what gets promoted.

Studying people's actions (what you can see, their history) is a good indicator of that—in fact, it is often the best indicator that cuts through any BS that might be pinned to some values poster created by HR. You want to know if your organization walks its talk?

More importantly—if you keep an open mind—it might provide some fresh insights.

Examples:

- Oscar worked at an investment bank. For all the talk about teamwork, diversity, collaboration, those that got promoted did one thing, and one thing only:

They brought in deals. And those that seemed to do it the fastest, broke rules, or did it the most ruthlessly got rewarded. And all were white guys.

- Grace sought to move from a technical to general management role at her life sciences firm. Studying everyone who made that transition, she found that you either spent some time in sales—or you were brought in from the outside. Those that got hired could communicate in the "language" of customers and not be bogged down in technical details.

- Katarina found that every new initiative not only had a key sponsor but, more importantly, had a moving story behind it. The first felt obvious to her, but the second actually challenged her approach to provide reams of data and evidence to make her case.

### Dig deep to get reality

When you conduct the Study Success exercise, maybe you find your company does promote humble team players—but you want to have some confirmation of that.

Make sure you dig deep: I've worked with clients in many of Silicon Valley's top tech firms: They are anything but flat meritocracies. Politics is alive and well there. My experience, and the research, would indicate that behind the scenes, someone had a sponsor, got visibility, provided things of value, or had those strong political skills.

Likewise, if a new leader comes in, go study their history. What did that leader do before, who are they a protégé of, or what is the first 90-day playbook for leaders at their past company? It's usually a great indication of what they will do.

One of my clients profusely thanked me after doing his homework. He discovered his new boss almost always cleared house when she took the reins at a new place. It was likely the CEO had hired her because she brought her former firm's playbook with her. So, when she came in acting nice and asking everyone to reveal their ambitions and vulnerabilities at an offsite, he was suspicious. His caution was merited— he survived and found a great lateral position while many of his peers got fired and ousted, one by one.

Back to Marta. Having made her Power Map, she was able to more easily identify and Study Success.

What she found:

- Those getting promoted in her region and headquarters were people who did not look like her. In her region, it was all men. In headquarters, no one from her region or an emerging market had ever made the leap.
- But aside from the obvious, what else did those who rose have in common that got them promoted?

In the region, those promoted to the leadership team had strong personal relationships with the president, spent a lot of time in the head office (ironic given a few of those very people were supposed to spend most of their time with customers, in the field), were very polished, and sounded definitive, even on things they knew they knew little about.

In headquarters, the last three promotions had been from within—people with technical and commercial chops and had served on several cross functional initiatives connected to a new product line.

Marta got depressed after studying who was successful at getting promoted.

Reality bites. But, as we will see in the next chapter, when she fed this information into the Probability Equation, that is what set her free.

**What to look for when you study success**

Study success by applying the skills of observation, asking good questions and triangulating any information you pick up. Ask yourself:

- What is the background of those that rose?
- What steps or path did they take to get there?
- How do they spend their time?
- With whom do they spend their time?
- How do they act and behave?

A distinct pattern may emerge. Sometimes you see two distinct groups, which is useful because it shows two potential paths or strategies used.

If you don't see anything you can replicate from their experience, that's good news too. It might mean (as you will see later) that you need to break rules or forge a different path).

**Empathy vs perspective taking**

We're advised to employ empathy. By walking in someone else's shoes, you can relate.

But the research shows we benefit more from perspective taking.

What's the difference? Empathy can cause us to relate too much to the other side. We can get caught up in how they will feel that we over-acquiesce or accommodate.

Perspective taking has you take the other side's perspectives because the key is to understand but not get sucked in.

Adam Galinsky's research in negotiations found that perspective takers could expand the pie and then secure what would benefit them. Perspective takers did better. Empathizers often just lose out.[93]

# CHAPTER 11

# The Probability Equation

*"Many people think that holding on and hanging in there are signs of great strength. But there are times when it takes much more strength to know when to let go —and then to do it."*
*– Ann Landers*

*"Just because you can, doesn't mean you should."*

A quiz:

There's an 80% chance a coin will always land on heads, and a 20% chance it will land on tails.

If I flip the coin, would you bet on heads or tails (assuming the payout is the same if it lands on heads or tails)?

Rethink your answer for a moment.

If you want to change your answer, do so now.

What did you decide?

This isn't a trick question.

If you bet on heads, you will be right 80% of the time. Even if you knew it would land on heads 51% of the time, that's odds you should take.

Yet it is surprising, when I work with many executives, that after assessing the odds, many of them place their bets on paths and strategies that have the lowest odds of success.

Why does this happen?

First, they go with their gut, intuition, what they think is right or based on some guru's video they came across surfing the web.

Second, they don't make a Power Map and scrutinize what success looks like in their organization. This means they don't know what the landscape looks like or what has worked. As Lincoln said, "What good does that do you?"

Not assessing your probability of success is like driving blind.

## Play the Percentages

If you are going to take a risk, take a calculated one. The smartest gamblers play the percentages. They know when to hold, fold, walk away or run, as the song by the late Kenny Rogers went. Calculating and playing the odds may not be sexy, or flashy, but if you win more than you lose, that sounds pretty good to me.

Which brings us to the Probability Equation and back to Marta.

It's clear when Marta did the "Study Success" exercise what the region and headquarters was promoting. And unless something changed radically from the past (which it did not in her case), her analysis was a pretty good indication of what was being rewarded.

To quickly recap:

- In the region, men were getting the nod. They also spent a lot of time in headquarters and presented commandingly.
- In headquarters, no emerging market employee had risen—but recent promotions had gone to those with technical skills, and to those who brought new business models.

If you are placing bets, knowing Marta was a Black woman, a minority in her region, what was her probability of success at getting promoted?

In the region, she placed the odds of getting promoted at under 5%. Looking at the leadership group, it wasn't even a group she wanted to be part of, nor would it help her with her longer-term goals. Five percent is something, but it's low. She could make all the moves in the world, but the odds were against her.

I'll be the first to say—which Marta found out—that the strategies that build power work faster and are more effective than you think. If she applied them boldly in this case, I'd say her chances would increase.

But just because they *can* work, doesn't mean it's worth the effort.

That is what the Probability Equation will make you think hard about. Plenty of people I work with keep believing and hoping their organizations will change. Sometimes you are better off going elsewhere or doing something radically different, like breaking the rules.

## Hope Is Not a Strategy

It boils down to considering three distinct strategies to achieve your goal:

**#1 Follow success. Do what the organization rewards.** Marta wasn't going to change her gender or the color of her skin. But she could be more political—blowing off the regional president, as she had done, had set the wrong impression. Never going to headquarters made her out of sight, out of mind. She could play that game more skillfully, and it would improve her odds of becoming the first Black woman being promoted.

**#2 Break the rules**. Marta could "stay in her lane," but now armed with her Power Map, she could reach out to key people, bring them value, and make her abilities known. That would involve leveraging strengths she had but was not using and getting creative, by building sources of power in novel ways, as you will see. Sometimes breaking the rules is the best way to get ahead.

**#3 Look elsewhere.** If the odds are low where you are at, go find out your market value. Marta was a sales star with strategic insight in a growing market. Yet she barely spoke to executive recruiters or updated her online profile. She felt it would not be loyal.

There is a fourth strategy: **Do nothing.**

You can hope things will change, but as I say to my clients: "Hope is not a strategy." This fourth strategy could, however, involve redefining your job, what you want, and the effort, trade offs, and risks involved. Most white-collar jobs are malleable, meaning you might have a job description and annual goals, but generally you can shape those in ways that best suit your interests, provided you still manage boss or organization expectations. And that may be okay for you.[94]

### Look before you leap

Most people are so frustrated in their companies that they immediately see the answer is moving to a new company.

That's a perfectly natural reaction. But take a step back before leaping. The grass is not always greener. We often overestimate how bad our situation is and underestimate the challenges on the outside.

**Key recommendations:**

**Examine options internally.** Sometimes you are in an area that is not growing, or where there is lots of competition, or maybe you are bored or have a weak boss. If there's no growth where you are, it's harder to move up! Look inside the company. Where is there growth? You should already have contacts inside and can set up conversations or even do side projects. Doing so helps you test the waters and makes coming to work more fun. One of my clients was set on leaving his company to find a job in Asia, but navigating internally found high growth opportunities in another division.

**Assess the market fully.** Don't cut the cord, only to find out there aren't jobs out there or the salaries are lower! Many technical people make the mistake believing they can leave to get a people-manager position elsewhere, but the fact is most companies want to hire people into people-manager roles, who have already done the role. So, an internal move into management is often easier. You might, of course, find the job market is awesome—and that's great because it increases your leverage and usually makes you bolder about asking your boss for a promotion.

**Use your company as a platform.** Even if you have decided to go, take advantage of all your company has to offer: training, attending industry events, projects that might add to your resume. Many companies have great brands, which can also get you speaking or publishing opportunities. Most employees who leave their companies tell me they regret not having built their network and personal brand more before leaving. To identify advantages of the "platform" you currently have, ask yourself: "If I left the company in three months, what would I no longer be able to do or access?"

**Don't burn bridges.** You may want to tell people off but be diplomatic—or might I dare say "political". More than one of my clients has returned to their company with a much higher and better position. Networks and reputation matter.

The good news is that the Power Map, Study Success, and Probability Equation can help you look smartly before you leap.

Where did Marta land on the three strategies?

Inside the region:

She could be more political and less dismissive (Strategy #1: Follow Success), but she was better off to Break the Rules and to Look Elsewhere. She was so busy keeping her head down producing great results that she had not checked her market value. Within three weeks of activating her LinkedIn profile, she had 20 companies reach out, four with attractive roles at higher salaries.

She had also studied powerful women who rose to the top in her country (a variation on "Study Success"). From that, she not only learned from their strategies to build power and rise, but it led her to reach out to them, which got a few recommending her for jobs. Exactly: Network and visibility.

By knowing her market value, she decreased her dependency on her company. In fact, for many of my clients, saying they are about to leave makes the company take action.

In headquarters:

The odds were low, but she could break rules to leap-frog into opportunities there. Despite no one from her market making it to headquarters, the group was promoting people inside, and who had a technical background. She could bring things of value, but she needed to be strategic.

Using her Power Map as a guide, she took action and broke some rules:

- **Asked the SVP**: The SVP was about three levels up. The SVP did know her, but it wasn't clear he knew her ambitions or what she could bring. Her Map made her see ways she could connect, and what would resonate with him. He cared about innovation and one new product line, and she had success with that. He liked to travel and cared about his future, and her region was the future that he should see. Getting him to mentor and sponsor her could accelerate her career.

- **Worked the network:** She asked a colleague who worked in headquarters, who she had met in a leadership program, for his advice. He quickly became an ally, and she asked him if he could raise her name and get her invited to a regional summit. He did, which gave her a forum for getting known by the two directors.

By looking outside the company, and knowing her market value, her confidence skyrocketed, which increased her willingness to make asks and be bolder inside. Her boss approved a trip to the regional summit and an important industry conference because she asked. The powerful women she had studied became her mentors. Not only did they flag her for job offers, one nominated her to be featured as a rising young leader to watch in a popular magazine, which did wonders for her brand.

She also got creative and created a top customer interview series. She saw how much the regional president enjoyed the media, and she used her strong customer relationships to record a Q&A with top customers. These video interviews were then featured by the marketing and PR department and got picked up by headquarters. Customer CEOs loved the attention. She invited the regional president to give opening remarks, where she said flattering words about him. It was a win for them, a win for her, and a win for the company—and was noticed back in headquarters.

Run down what builds power, and what Marta did:

- Political Skills
- Network and Relationships
- Visibility and Brand
- Presence and Communication
- Control of Hard Resources

Check. Check. Check. Check. Check.

Her "hard power" accrued as well: She got a budget to make the customer interviews more professional, headquarters asked her to join a worldwide task force, and she became the main liaison for the region.

Don't forget that Marta was smart, worked hard, and was knowledgeable. But without taking the actions we described, she'd still be frustrated.

As a result, she was feeling more in command, confident, and in the driver's seat. And spoiler alert: she got promoted although the pandemic meant she would first work remotely from her region.

While it took effort, she actually felt she was working *more efficiently*. Because opportunities were now coming to her, and she was focused on what moved the needle, she actually worked less. That gave her team an opportunity to step up, and it gave her an opportunity to add people and start to actually implement many great initiatives that she had not been able to before.

That's powerful.

You've now had a sneak peek at The Snowball (tactics), but everything was put in motion by first getting real and getting strategic.

To fully understand what tactics to start with—and what not to start with—let's now turn to The Snowball.

**How risky is it to break the rules? 想办法!**

"Breaking the rules" sounds risky, but remember you are taking calculated risks, especially when you understand the power landscape.

Breaking the rules is nothing more than harnessing the principles of how you build power, often in ways other people haven't thought of, or are too timid to do:

One executive interviewed the C-suite, 3 levels up, as part of an executive education program on leadership (an assignment he thought up). This played to their egos, gave him visibility, and built relationships. After that, they all knew him, and surprise: One put him on a high-profile project.

An introverted IT executive was resigned to the fact that his ideas would never see the light of day because of a blocking boss. He identified the head of strategy as a power player, whose team he could see joining. He realized they were both runners, so he set up a company marathon training club—knowing only the two of them would join. Lots of talk time.

An executive leading a sustainability initiative reached out to local media, which got her company and the concept press. That drew the attention of others, got her a post in an industry association and leadership position on a business roundtable, which led to a following online, which got her connected to a worldwide think tank. These became a source of power, and it got her company to pay attention—and back a pilot.

Many prominent groundbreakers have publicly said they do not "stay in their lane." They understand how to build power, and they go do it. If you feel you are disadvantaged, you are probably going to have to try some new things, to break rules.

The Chinese say "想办法" (Xiang ban fa), Come up with a way. Indeed.

## Do birds of a feather flock together?

Yes, they do. Research shows we are attracted to those that are like us.

The problem is most of us see similarity too narrowly. They think you have to be the same gender or race.

Most of my clients—women, minorities, immigrants—have very little in common, on the surface, with their bosses or leadership. Example: "I'm a female Indian immigrant who has an accent, grew up watching cricket, and celebrates other holidays. What could I possibly have in common with the white male leaders that all studied at Auburn?"

The solution: Broaden what you have in common. Consider hobbies, shared experiences, your current situation. That Indian client bonded with the Marketing VP because their kids were obsessed with Fortnite and Tik Tok, and the two had originally studied engineering but moved into new disciplines.

The research says almost any bit of similarity can form a bond. Even mimicry—deliberately mirroring someone's body language during a conversation (you lean back after they do, you cross your legs after they do), has been shown to predispose people to us.

We've seen how building relationships with your team, adversaries, diverse weak ties—but particularly those with power—is so critical to advancement. So, tap into similarity.

You may be more birds of the same feather than you think.

# PART III
# The Snowball

"Nothing happens unless something moves."

– Albert Einstein

You've discovered The Rock to Get Real. You know the hard truth of politics and power in organizations, and your eyes have been opened to the fallacy of the "Kumbaya" school of leadership that says, authenticity, transparency, vulnerability, and a servant mentality will advance you in the modern organization.

And, you now have a tool—The Map—that helped you Get Strategic. It gives clarity and guides you toward your goal. It makes you more strategic and deliberate about where you spend your time.

## Summary

Knowing the truth and having a plan are great, but they point you to actions you need to take. An action, as we know, is what puts things in motion.

Like a snowball rolling down a hill, you will gain momentum—but first you need to give it a push.

# CHAPTER 12

# Building the Snowball

## THE SNOWBALL

Kids are very clear on how to build a giant snowball:

- Finding slightly wetter snow helps.
- They start small and start rolling—they don't try to pack it too much.
- Then once they've got a basic ball, the snowball gets bigger, fast—but at a certain point, it helps to have a friend, or a downward slope, to help keep it moving.

Building power to advance toward your goals is the same. You need:

- **Conditions:** Start where you've got better chances for success. Think of that old saying, "S/he doesn't have a snowball's chance in hell."

- **Action:** Start small and start doing. Einstein wasn't lying when he said, "Nothing happens until something moves."

- **Momentum:** Adjust, build, grow. Once you gain traction, things *get easier* as your power *grows exponentially.* Attending to the snowball, you become unstoppable.

Fail to follow these three steps, and it's unlikely you will make that giant, powerful snowball—unlikely you will achieve your big, ambitious goal.

You already have gotten a glimpse of the great things that can happen when you take action.

Recall a few of them:

- John, the product manager, who identified and raised his hand to lead a cross-functional initiative.
- Sam, the quiet associate brand manager, who let her boss know of her ambitions, started to speak up in meetings, and used her quantitative skills to fill a void.
- Victor, the innovator, who "bumped" into the leader most likely to sponsor him, leveraged the press, and reshaped the metrics by which he and his bosses were judged by.
- And of course, Marta, the ambitious territory manager, who leapfrogged into a senior role by connecting with key people there and by testing the job market.

You might be thinking: This seems too good to be true! What's the catch?

Marta, in her own words:

> *"I couldn't believe how fast things happened. It was much easier than I thought. Sure, I needed to put in the work and face some of my fears. Not everything worked, of course, but most of it did. And it worked extremely—no, surprisingly— well. I'm feeling more confident than ever, more empowered, more in control."*

What's the catch? It's simple: If you don't do anything, nothing will happen.

---

**Prune your tomatoes**

My clients are driven, "type A" personalities. They put a premium on working hard and delivering.

But that also gets them into trouble: They get overwhelmed because they feel they need to deliver on everything and respond to everything

If you hear yourself saying "I've got too much on my plate," can't turn down any request, and as a result can't focus, think about pruning the tomatoes.

For a tomato plant to really take off and produce great fruit, it benefits from being pruned. You basically pinch the "suckers," specific shoots. That allows other branches to grow; they get more energy, and you get bigger, better harvest.

242 | MICHAEL WENDEROTH

How are you spending your time? Are you spread too thin? What do you need to stop doing, so you can spend more time on something else that is important?

You may need to say "no" more or "strategically quit." Seth Godin, in *The Dip*, says this beautifully. People quit when it's painful and stick to things when they can't be bothered. Maybe you feel guilty saying no, or just sending an email is so easy, or you feel important being asked to help. But these yesses add up and fracture our time.

Ever notice how powerful people say "no" a lot, how they carefully guard their time—but also don't make you feel bad when they turn you down?

You can too—in fact, you need to if you want to advance.

What might you need to say no to—to stop doing—to free up time? Quitting might mean growing.

Prune the tomatoes, so you get better fruit.

Let's look at how Marta created the snowball, which took her from frustrated to unstoppable:

1) **Conditions: Start where you have better chances for success**
Marta already completed this step when she made her Power Map, conducted the Study Success exercise, and ran the Probability Equation.

So, good news if you have been applying the exercises in Part II to your current situation: You've already set yourself up for success.

For Marta, the conditions weren't great for getting promoted in her region, but the conditions were slightly better for leapfrogging into headquarters. The job market for her skills was great. In fact, interviewing kept her sharp and made her entertain the possibility of starting her own distributorship. Many companies seemed to need help in the region.

To leapfrog into headquarters, Marta needed to get visibility and show her value in headquarters—but build relationships with specific people. Her Power Map showed her *who* mattered, *where* she could start (influence conduits), and *what* mattered (influence assets).

The exact *how* was missing. What step to start with? For example, what did "becoming visible" actually mean she should do? How could she get the SVP to see what value she could bring to the team?

2) **Action: Start small and start doing**
Most executives I work with are smart—sometimes too smart for their own good. They overcomplicate things. They go into analysis paralysis.

Really, you just need to start somewhere. The Rock has already made you aware of what you need. And the

244 | MICHAEL WENDEROTH

Map has given you a great guide. You have increased the probabilities dramatically.

Hoping the snowball will magically form is like hoping everyone will see your great work and suddenly promote you: It's just daydreaming.

Marta needed to take action.

The quickest and simplest way to be known by the SVP was to reach out directly.

In a conversation, she could let him know her ambition, propose insights, learn more about what mattered to him. It should not be too hard as she was already on his radar. He had sponsored her for a global leadership program and sent her a congratulatory award for her sales achievement. But she did not want to assume that meant anything.

She balked: I can't be that bold. Who is a territory manager to reach out three levels up? What if he says no? Her mind ran through all the reasons why she should or could not ask. (Sound familiar? Recall the Ask Experiment in Chapter 8.)

She contemplated other things she could do, like asking her colleague in the leadership program to introduce her to one of the direct reports, meet her, maybe present an insight at a regional meeting that would stand out.

Often the fastest way between point A and B (her and the SVP) *is* a straight line. Of course, going through the colleague, a direct report, or another "influence conduit" might be necessary to pave the way.

We considered the upside, and the worst-case scenario, if she reached out directly. If the SVP said no, it might mean he had zero interest. But he might share why. The clarity of an answer would be liberating. She wouldn't be wondering and spinning her wheels.

Marta had a direct opportunity—and when you have it, take it. She had access, and access was power. Seize the opportunity! That's not to say she couldn't approach her colleague and advance on that front too (she did).

She took the "risk" and asked for a 1-1 meeting. She asked if they could speak as she wanted to thank him personally for sponsoring her, and she wanted to seek his career advice.

He said he would be delighted to.

In their conversation, she offered some distribution insights and invited him to see her distributor network if he came to the region and if he could mentor her. He said yes to everything.

## Landing that meeting—and making it work

Of course, Marta planned how to have that initial conversation with the SVP, and how to ask. She needed to make it simple for him, meaningful, and provide a compelling reason. She also needed to be clear. It wasn't that hard, but it did take planning.

Two things helped Marta and can help you:

Landing the meeting: How should she reach out and get a "yes"? One of simplest ways is to flip things around and ask if a person two levels below you reached out. What would compel you to say yes or be willing to meet for 15 minutes?

Sticking the landing: Most people spend far too much time on engineering how to meet, and not nearly enough time on how they want the meeting to end. Plan what you want to achieve, how you will open, focus, and close.[95]

To be clear, any of the actions she had laid out, like going indirectly through his top direct reports, would have moved her forward—far more than doing nothing.

Return to the Power Map. The last step is the most important: listing and committing to three actions you will take, in the next week, to advance toward your goals.

As you assess which actions are best to start with, consider the following:

**Leverage a strength:** You probably already have some unique sources of power, so start by using them first. Marta had won sales awards, and many of her distribution insights had been adopted in the region.

Elena wanted to get promoted but felt awkward about telling her boss. She had deep, long-standing relationships all around her, so she started by approaching two trusted VPs, who influenced her boss, to get their advice—to get them on her side.

Phil had just joined a global firm and was starting a new internal consulting unit. He worked in an emerging niche, so he first approached a powerful HR business partner head to propose presenting insights in the leadership training and orientation for high potentials. That quickly put him in direct contact with all the company's up and comers—and their sponsors.

**"Piggyback" on top of something you already do:** You're busy, so take advantage of something you do already.

Marisa worked in the headquarters of a global bank but was seen as a good manager who got information for the C-Suite. She had constant contact with all the regions and had to coordinate many meetings. Taking advantage of that, she started to collect insights—innovative ideas or common challenges. She kept it simple and turned it into a weekly insights newsletter, which she sent to the C-Suite or mentioned in casual hallway conversations, focusing on who might care about what insight the most. Before long, many of those leaders sought her out, which changed her reputation, built her brand, and made it easier for her to identify, or in fact in her case, create a senior role for her to move into.

**Even tiny actions, repeated, can make a huge difference:** We think we need to knock it out of the park with a home run, but a bunch of singles (baseball analogy) will also bring in a run.

Marisa, in our previous example, kept cranking out the insights letter. It was easy for her and, in fact, led her to follow-up to ask great questions or get more insights. It can take time for the impact to register.

Alex discovered that bringing cookies to meetings and creating a casual atmosphere was creating an impression that he was a secretary, which contributed to him not being "seen" as a leader. He rotated the role of bringing snacks, stepped up his attire, sent out an email before the meeting with the agenda and his expectations and assigned a different person to take notes and send him the summary afterwards. That maintained collegiality but quickly shifted how he was seen, particularly when powerful leaders dropped in on the sessions.

Starting new habits or changing a habit can be hard—things get ingrained. Heads down worked for you, so networking initially seems like a burden.

The recommendation to keep things simple and piggyback on top of existing habits? Straight from BJ Fogg at Stanford, an expert in habit formation.[96] By repeating these actions, each time it gets easier—and you start to reprogram yourself.

## Where NOT to Start

When you are picking your first actions, here's what to avoid:

**Doing the hardest thing possible:** Pat had a really hard time confronting her boss. She could be long-winded; her boss went straight to the point. Her boss was also impossible to schedule with and always showed up late. But Pat had amazing sponsors, who in fact influenced her boss. But Pat didn't want to tap into those sponsors—didn't feel like it would be fair—and insisted on confronting her boss. But the thought stressed her out so much that she did nothing.

**Create when you can leverage:** Jian thought he needed to create a conference to impress everyone around him—the thought exhausted him. When we examined his weekly activities, he discovered he ran an important bi-weekly meeting but had a junior person to send out the summary. He didn't need to do anything fancy to garner visibility and get meetings—he simply could have used that summary himself to call for 1-1 meetings with key people, to turn it into a stronger platform, like Marisa had.

Likewise, Carolina tied herself into a knot looking for second and third order contacts to influence a key SVP. When she made her Power Map, she realized she overlooked the SVP's executive assistant, who was her former boss. Speaking to that assistant unlocked insights and opened the door.

**Go after your toughest critics and adversaries:** It is said you should keep your friends close and enemies closer, but trying to turn all those enemies overnight is hard, and exhausting. Back to Pat. She was bugged by a peer of hers on the leadership team, who really had it out for her, and focused her energies trying to change that relationship. That peer didn't really matter and could have been neutralized by enlisting her sponsors and bringing enough neutral people to her side.

Don't try to be fancy because it may lead you to doing nothing, and when there's no action, there is no movement. Think of doing experiments, what you can learn. Take some calculated risk.

3) **Momentum: adjust, build, grow. Once you get traction and the general idea, it all actually gets easier, as power grows exponentially.**
   We saw how Marta's confidence quickly grew: When the SVP said yes, the meeting led to an introduction to his top report and monthly 1-1 mentoring. That made her increasingly comfortable asking and engaging in behaviors and strategies that built her power. She then started to advocate for herself. Two weeks later she convinced her boss to appoint her to represent the region at an internal worldwide summit, which got her more visibility. And that emboldened her to create the executive forum interview series, which really propelled her reputation. The snowball grew.

   Those actions provided value to others, generated new insights, and brought others to her side, which ultimately made pushing the Snowball easier. The top team in headquarters saw her as valuable, and her stock rose. That led the regional president to want to support her, or at least not cross her, as it made him look good in the eyes of the SVP. When she got featured in the press, everyone took note—inside the region, by headquarters, and by tons of recruiters.

To keep a snowball big and growing remember what kids do—they get help from a slope or have friends push too. Here's how to translate that insight:

**Seek permanence**: It's tiring to constantly come up with reasons to meet people 1-off. Look to create a recurring mechanism with some institutional permanence, one that creates value for others, with you at the center or in the key brokering position. Marta's "executive forums" are a great example—it constantly created a flow of diverse, important people, generated visibility, and she held a key position. Moreover, she got the budget, and the PR team did the marketing. After running several events, network effects kicked in. The event was a fixed feature, and no one else could copy it.

**Create forcing functions**: Willpower is overrated, so find what I call forcing functions. Marta's executive forums are a good example. Ongoing mentorship, through monthly meetings, means you will always see a key person. Marisa's weekly insights letter became a habit, forcing her to focus weekly on this productive activity.

**Address your "gating factor"**: When I conduct 360 reviews, I look for the gating factor, the single biggest factor that prevents someone from going to the next level. You will have to address that at some point. For one executive I worked with, it was her communication skills—how she showed up. We did exercises to address her worst habits, but she harnessed other sources of power to help her. Her sponsors also coached her. She used social proof—receiving awards in an executive education program and highlighting that—to enhance her brand, predisposing people to see her as powerful.

**Deal with jealousy and not being liked**: If the other kids see you and a popular kid working together, and your snowball is growing really big, most people will come to your side and want to be associated with you. When Marta was seen as a rising star, it was sure her regional president began to see advantages to promoting her.

**Track progress**: You've got big goals, but break them down into manageable parts. Track progress and set up measures to track yourself against your past self.[97] This helps you see progress, which is a source of motivation. With clients, we often track inputs (actions they take) and outputs (actions we can objectively see, to see if they are rising). One way to track if you are becoming more powerful, for example, is to see if other people come to you for advice or favors.

**How not to become someone else's stepping stone**

"I created this great event, but then a cunning peer came in and got all the benefits (exposure, network, credit)!"

As we discussed before, don't become a doormat— or steppingstone. Create value but also make sure you claim value.

Ways to make sure you benefit from what you do:

**Remember the Rock:** Barabasi (5 Laws of Success) makes it clear that in group work, usually one person is credited as the leader. If that matters to you, take note! Beware: Research also shows that women who write articles with men often get less credit, so take facts like that into consideration.

**Be assertive and make sure you have allies:** Be clear on what you want. Knowing others might take credit behind closed doors, build allies who will speak up for you or defend you. Be clear what are key roles you need to maintain.

**Don't trust blindly:** Not everyone has purity of intent. Before you team up, do little experiments, each one testing for trust, and act accordingly. As you gain power, you will gain hard resources which can be used as carrots, or sticks.

> **Socialize your idea:** Sometimes the best defense is a good offense. Socialize your idea early, so it is clear where ownership came from. Sometimes a rival's source of power is being able to copy your idea and scale it more quickly, so you may need to move fast.

Marta had built a powerful snowball, and the top recurring mechanisms (the ongoing mentoring, the executive forums, representing her region at a key monthly global meeting) kept her moving:

- She gained profound realizations on what she could do to advance her cause and felt better about herself.
- She found it easier to get things done.
- She got promoted, which further propelled her.

Before you know it, you've become unstoppable.

## Apply the Snowball to Your Networking

Back when I started writing about building power, my editor at *Harvard Business Review* wanted me to focus on networking. She said so many readers struggled with it. That forced me to address key topics blocking people.

I've got extensive exercises I use with clients—for example deep mapping and auditing your network—but here's the 4 practical steps you need to take to get started:

## 1) Shift your mindset by getting curious—and getting moving

Master networker Keith Ferrazzi hits this point home in *Never Eat Alone*.[98] Think about being *interested* in others. Thinking about networking as a self-serving chore pulls many people back. Research in the U.S. and Italy by Tiziana Casciaro found that people who approached networking with excitement, curiosity, and an open mind networked significantly more than those who viewed it as dirty, self-serving, a necessary evil or chore.[99] It's having that growth mindset: Change how you think, and it can help change how you act. Consider how your networking can benefit others (like your team, the larger organization, or even the other person) to power yourself.

Second, if you are chained to your desk all day, nothing will happen. (While the pandemic has made personal contact more difficult, we discovered new ways to connect, for example, "I'm disappointed the conference was canceled, but it looks like we all now have all the travel and session time returned to us... I would love to connect for 15 minutes because I was really looking forward to your insight on this particularly topic, which we're seeing all across our industry.")

## 2) Make a simple list

Everything starts with a plan. Write down 10 people, and how you can reach out and meet them. Does that list have breadth, connectivity, and dynamism?

If that's daunting, start with one of these three approaches:

- **Pick a few "dormant" ties**: These are people like a former colleague that you used to know well. Because you have a shared history, they are likely to say yes to a catch-up. But since you have not been in touch for a long time, they are now a weak tie, with new perspectives and information.

- **Tap into alumni networks**: People are more willing to help others like them (similarity and identity).

- **Ask and multiply**: That first dormant tie or alumni you speak to? At the end of the conversation, tell them how insightful it was—and who else in their network they could recommend and introduce, who would provide powerful insights on a specific topic.

## 3)  5 simple levers to get people to say "yes" to meeting

The challenge is powerful people are busy and have less incentive to meet people they don't know well or perceive as less useful.

Conduct a simple exercise: If ten junior employees in your company reached out to you for a coffee, but you could only meet one, who would you pick and why? Chances are you just generated strategies you can use.

Chances are it was one of these five:

- **Come recommended**: As discussed above.

- **Play up similarities**: Remember birds of a feather—look for any similarity.

- **Bring value**: Drop an insight of why or what makes you valuable—remember what top salespeople do.

- **Use flattery:** Hey, it works. It might have a point of diminishing returns, but I have yet to have found that point.

- **Ask and be persistent:** You won't know unless you ask, and the one that asked in person concisely and had done their homework, instead of with a mass email, was really hard to say no to.

## 4) Deepen the networking

Once you get started, ways to supercharge your network:

- **Identify and target "super connectors":** Which of your contacts has historically introduced you to other key people? These super connectors, says Brian Uzzi, are powerful and under-examined.

- **Become a connector:** Where can you become a connector, fill a gap? Many people create events in their organizations, which allows them to invite interesting and diverse people in. That puts you at the center of the action. Done well, it means you don't have to push into other people's networks; it causes others to come to you.

- **Deep experiences**: All work and no play makes for a dull day, so bonding with people outside the work routine can build a more potent network. Activities that evoke some passion, lead to interdependence, and have meaning are most effective. It's why the running club we saw earlier, or why group offsite activities, are so effective. Get creative, and you might actually learn to love networking.

Strong networks don't just happen. Take these steps to carefully construct yours.

# CHAPTER 13

# Dangerous Avalanche Ahead?

*"Most people can bear adversity; but if you wish to know what a man [sic] really is give him power."*
*– Robert Green Ingersoll*

When I proposed the Rock-Map-Snowball as my framework, a good friend told me bluntly that the snowball was a bad metaphor.

"I get it," he said. "Snowballs grow bigger and bigger."

But he added: "But snowballs can get out of control and destroy."

My first reaction was where the heck did you grow up? The Rocky Mountains where you had a snowball roll down a hill and take out a small house?

But he had a point that I needed to consider.

Power is nothing more than a force. You can use it to get more of what you want done, and what "end" you want is a personal choice. You can use power to destroy, or you can use it to build. You can use it to advance others, causes, projects, yourself, or all of these. What's the end you want?

The fundamental question is: Does power really corrupt? Will it turn you from a well-meaning, thoughtful person into an arrogant, narcissistic jerk?

There is solid research that should give us pause.

Recall the story of Jane Elliot, a school teacher from Iowa. In 1968, she did a small experiment, so her class could experience racism. She divided them by eye color and told the one group that they were better and smarter because of their eye color. She praised them, gave them more privilege, and spoke down to the other set of kids.

The children's behavior changed fairly quickly: The ones who were told they were better started acting that way, even putting the other kids down, justifying they were better. Being told they were more powerful got them acting more powerfully, which led to more power. The other group became more timid. This created a self-reinforcing system.

Later, she flipped the roles. The same thing happened, but in reverse.

The research helps explain why. There are disinhibiting effects that come from power. It can lead to illusions of control and "disillusions of grandeur."[100] Studies show the more powerful we get, the more self-centered and arrogant we can become, which can lead to overestimating our abilities—and underestimating external factors or the abilities of others. All of which can lead to taking more risk, feeling above reproach, to disregarding others.[101]

Less powerful people are likely to be more cautious and even shy away from some of the very behaviors—like asking, asserting, building a network—that would help them. The powerful get more powerful; the powerless get less. The research explains how power hierarchies reinforce themselves.[102]

*Note that I said "can" lead to. Our fates are not ordained.*

The solution is to make sure you get outside perspectives—that ensures you don't get too arrogant and over-confident. At the same time, go too far and you become overaccommodating.

There are some simple ways to keep yourself in check.

## Are You Icarus?

Before examining what measures we can take, I want to address why I did not stress this dark side of power at the very beginning of the book when we were on the Rock?

The first reason is that most of us already have this deeply held belief about power leading to evil (see Myth #2 in Chapter 3).

The second, and more important reason, is that people are so far from losing control, it's not even close. If we think of a scale from 1-10, with 1 being doing nothing that will build power and 10 being doing everything, most people are well south of a 3. Excessively warning them causes people to be even more cautious—and then do nothing. They won't even experiment.

The old story warns of Icarus flying too close to the sun, causing him to plummet to earth. The truth is most people haven't even gotten off the ground.

---

**Learning from dictators, cult leaders, and fraudsters**

We're dismissive of cunning politicians and con artists, but if you study how they come to power, you see all the principles of building power at work.

Look at Theranos, the multi-billion biotech startup headed by Stanford graduate Elizabeth Holmes. John Carreyou documents the story in his book, *Bad Blood*.

Holmes used her prestigious affiliations to generate trust and brand, built a network of top venture capitalists, garnered favorable press, and created a narrative with media support. She got momentum and purged those who spoke against her. Many people followed her. In her case, it all came crashing down—but very late and at very serious costs.

Think about how that playbook can work for you, bring power—and what you will do with it when you have it.

How do we keep the "dark sides" of power in check? There are what I call personal and structural strategies, the most important being:

## Personal strategies:

**Set up "trip wires":** What if there was an alarm bell that went off when you hit, on the scale we described earlier, a 5, 6, 7,8, or 9, which would indicate you were getting close to a 10? Create "trip wires" by writing down visible signs or behaviors that you should flag you—and make you pause. Make sure to write it down because we have bad memories. In the future, you probably won't have as much perspective. I also recommend writing down now what you will do with all that power you get when you have it. At the very least, reading your note will cause you to reflect. If you believe you'll cross ethical lines, write down all those ethical trip wires.

**Walk around:** Powerful people can isolate themselves and can get surrounded by people who tell them what they want to hear. So, literally build your schedule, so you see and hear what other people in the organization are experiencing through skip level discussions, shadowing, or casual conversations. A diverse network also includes people below you.

**Have an empowered co-pilot:** Between 1970 and 1990, Korean Air went through a disproportionate series of tragic plane crashes. It turns out the copilots saw the accidents coming but said nothing, fearing that would infuriate the pilot. A big part of the solution was changing the language of the cockpit to English, which in this case allowed the pilot and copilot to escape hierarchical norms more common in Korean culture. The bigger lesson is that you can avoid mistakes if people feel free to speak up (Amy Edmondson calls this having an environment of "psychological safety"— for example hospitals got better results when nurses could challenge doctors without backlash).

Get a copilot who will tell you the truth, and don't cut off their head if they do.

### Hire a hacker?

When I gained a reputation for helping people get promoted, and I started sharing and speaking the truth (The Rock) to companies, I was surprised when a senior leader reached out.

He told me, bluntly: "I heard your talk, and there is so much truth there. You actually do know all the real ways—not the BS advice—that gets people promoted. In fact, if I'm honest, I did many of them."

At this point most people then lambast me for sharing this truth. But what came next bowled me over: "I think of you like a hacker. You know how to exploit the system because you know its flaws [his words], and you know where it is badly designed. So, I want you to come in and tell my leaders how to address those flaws."

Who better than to fix your problems than a hacker? If we know how the system works, we can employ sound structural strategies to keep the worst excesses in check.

## Structural Strategies:

You don't need my exhaustive list.

Conduct the same exercise I do with many clients:

After reading this book, or even better, after having risen and built power, make a list of the most important levers and actions you took that led you to rise.

Now, ask yourself if you could design the organization so that the levers you used would be rendered ineffective, what would you do?

There are many structural things we can do to improve organizations—but as I said at the beginning, you need to deeply understand why and how things operate. To fix a system, you need to understand how the system works.

A few examples:

- Those who speak more and take up more airtime are remembered, or might "look stronger". Fix: Change the way meetings are run. People submit ideas on paper, the ideas read out without attribution, and people can then chime in but are given 2 minutes and speaking order is randomly chosen. This may neutralize excessive attention on one person, encourage silent voices to be heard, and has been shown to lead to better decisions.

- Likewise, revisit your promotion process and hiring process. Even look at how opportunities are "advertised" (most are not—they go through informal ties, so maybe they should be?)

Once power is lodged, it can be self-reinforcing and hard to dismantle. Power structures can be upset, but that requires: 1) those with less power building (or taking) their own power, and 2) understanding how the system works. I'm not so optimistic those in power will change the system that clearly benefits them.

**Re-read this chapter when you excessively LEK!**

What's Lekking?

Lekking, a term from the animal world, occurs when animals, mainly males, strut their stuff to gain attention.

Research by Arjit Chatterjee and Donald Hambrick studied hundreds of CEOs, analyzing company annual reports. The more "lekking behavior" they found, the more likely the leader would favor big bold potentially damaging actions—but in general did not guarantee great performance.

How did they detect lekking? The size of the leader's photograph, the number of times they referred to themselves, prominence in press articles and their compensation levels relative to others in the firm. One of the big lekkers was Ken Lay, the CEO of Enron.

There's a lot of room between being invisible and hogging all the attention.

But if you have a way to examine your communications, maybe you can set a trip wire to detect excessive lekking—a trip wire that says go back and reread this chapter.[103]

# CHAPTER 14

# The Real Danger You Face

You could get too close to the sun like Icarus, but it's more likely that you haven't even left the ground. Plus, you now have some strategies to monitor if you go too high…

But the real danger preventing you from succeeding is not flying too high.

The real danger is on the next page.

Did you see it on the previous page?

Did you hold up the mirror and take a deep look at what will hold you back?

## That's Right: The Real Danger Is You

The real danger is not some dark side, of losing control, of a snowball careening out of control.

The real danger is that you will self-sabotage. That you will get in your own way and do something that keeps you from building that snowball. Period.

Remember that the myths are really strong. Remember that everyone else out there watches those feel-good videos and parrots the same advice.

If you've been reading critically, you should already know what is likely to sabotage you.

But here they are again and what you need to make sure they don't happen.

**The eight ways you will sabotage your own progress:**

1) **You don't do:** Nothing happens until something moves. What is the logic by which your current strategy is working? How do you expect to change anything if you don't do anything? Many clients are, to use Samuel Beckett's wonderful phrase, "Waiting

for Godot" (for something that will never happen). Hope is not a strategy.

2) **You become happy with a small win—and stop building the snowball:** Only you define success. If you have no destination, any road can lead you there. So, write down what you really want. What's the big goal? Remember what poet Mary Oliver wrote, "Tell me, what is it you plan to do with your one wild and precious life?" Remember that getting a meeting with a key person is not the same as sponsorship. Someone introducing you to another key person is not the same as them handing you power.

3) **You got burned:** Did you really get burned? Not everything works 100 percent of the time, but what did you learn? Remember that we often need to try on new behaviors to grow, and that can feel uncomfortable. Think of your actions as experiments. If your boss says no way in a million years will you ever get promoted, you've certainly got a lot of clarity.

4) **You got burned out:** You started the snowball, but you didn't build momentum. Build recurring mechanisms, forcing functions, enlist allies that will help power you.

5) **You got complacent:** Set big goals but also small ones, and track—both so you feel accomplishment, but also so you know what the bigger goal is. And because you can lose perspective when you have power, many powerful people take their foot off the gas and stop

doing the very things—networking, brand building, using hard power—that make them successful.

6) **You can't get over wanting to be liked:** You crave it; it's that Kumbaya thing. You can't stand someone saying something negative about you or a snooty comment. Get over it. As Jeff Pfeffer loves to quote, CEO Gary Loveman, "If you want to be liked, get a dog." Sure, there's a balance you need between warmth and competence. But that same person that laughed or dismissed you generally changes their tune when they see you have power.

7) **You abdicate your power:** When you examine your sources of power, you will find ones you have but aren't even using. That's one of the top issues Ron Carucci discovered in a study of what sunk new leaders in transition.[104] The problem they had wasn't exercising their power—it was abdicating it. Many didn't want to seem bossy, or wanted to be overly inclusive, so they did not take action. You may also be abdicating your power to create—creating sources of power, as you have seen, is much easier than you think.

8) **You didn't get help:** Willpower is overrated, and these skills can be hard to adopt on our own. Personal change is not always easy. A good proxy is to think about how good you are at keeping to a challenging regimen in other aspects of your life (exercise, time management, a diet, for example). Maybe you do need a trainer, a coach, or peer help. But get someone good, someone who really understands the evidence

274 | MICHAEL WENDEROTH

around power and not going to feed you feel-good life coaching platitudes.

So, if you really want to know what will hold you back, these are the top eight that I see.

These are the things that will really stop you from getting promoted.

> **Dealing with setbacks**
>
> You don't get the job, a peer stabs you in the back, you get derailed, you lose confidence, you believe you will never recover.
>
> As you rise, you are inevitably going to face setbacks. Your job is to stay resilient and make sure they don't stop you.
>
> Most advice says to focus and reflect on what you may have done wrong and how you would do it over again if you had to.
>
> That's helpful—but we can take that too far and blame ourselves.
>
> Shift your perspective and go through the 3 P's:
>
> **Personalization:** You can take some responsibility, but you don't have to blame yourself for everything. There's a bigger picture. Not everything happens to us because of us.

**Pervasiveness:** You're likely to see the failure extends to other areas of your life, or work. Because I failed at this, everything I do is a failure. One setback does not a career make.

**Permanence:** Recall the growth mindset. Learn, and that makes you stronger. More people have been derailed than you possibly think. Are you going to use that as an excuse or as information?

Asking yourself these questions to increase your resilience to bounce back faster—and stronger.[105]

If you have decided you can learn political skills and build power on your own, I trust this book has been a helpful, if not a thought provoking, resource.

But I urge you to set several "trip wires." Write down now what would indicate in two months that you are *not* advancing toward your goals and building power. If you see those red flags, consider getting help.

Many people seek expert coaching when it's too late, when their pain is acute, or worse, they have already been derailed. My coaching engagements run 6-12 months because change takes time. There may be quick wins, but there are no magic bullets.

## Why powerlessness corrupts

We're told that power corrupts, but I encourage you to think about the opposite:

*How not having power corrupts.*

Say power and most people think about Machiavelli, the dark arts, narcissists, and workplace bullies. But if you look at the definition—a force that enables you to get things done—there is nothing inherently bad about power. Given that power is invisible but omnipresent in all social relationships, it behooves us to understand how it works, how to build it, how to defend against, and how we might use it to get more done.

I liken power to fire. Know how to use it, you can channel it to illuminate a city or power a metropolis. Use it indiscriminately, you can burn the whole place down.

But you can do neither of the above, or will have a *much harder time doing so*, if you don't have any power. If you don't have any power, you are forced or might have to go along with the wishes of others. If you accept that you have no power and choose not to build power, you are helpless.

Power might corrupt, but...

*Powerlessness corrupts.*

Think about what you can do if you have more power: get more things done, be in control of your time and career, maybe even change policies within your organization, be able to support and uplift others who need it and be a role model to others.

The playing field within organizations is not fair. There is bias and inequity. Power is rarely given.

You need to take it. Instead of waiting for change, do something about it: Be an agent. Understand how to build power.

# CHAPTER 15

# Conclusion and Next Steps

I believe in the evidence, and I've worked with countless executives through their transformations.

But you can't simply read an academic study and figure out how to apply those concepts in your career. That's why I've distilled those strategies down into the actionable advice and exercises in this book.

Embrace these strategies and understand the ways you can use them to propel yourself forward in your career.

The reality is that the workplace is not a meritocracy. The world is not fair. And hard work and doing a good job, while they may have helped you get you this far, are not enough to help you advance further.

Instead, embrace power. Once you realize this hard truth, you stop doing the things that really won't help you achieve your goals and instead focus on what really moves the needle as far as advancement and promotions.

Apply the lessons in this book, and you will:

- Apply a playbook that focuses on the areas and strategies that will propel you, covering critical political skills, networking, visibility and branding, executive presence and communications.
- Become more adept at identifying what brings power, leveraging valuable resources you already possess, and creating new ones.
- Have more confidence in advocating for yourself. When confidence kicks in, you become energized and unstoppable.
- Become more strategic and focused. You'll probably get more things done with less effort and be more pleasant to be around because politics and power no longer faze you.

As a result, you will:

- Receive promotions, new challenges, new job offers, bigger bonuses, and more resources—making it easier to get things done.
- Have more career options because you have a more powerful position and reputation and know the right people. Opportunities will start to come to you, which gives you more freedom, choice, and control.
- Have a seat at the decision-making table, which enables you to shape direction, policy, and culture.
- Have a stronger sense of self-worth now that you are valued and have been recognized. You are now moving up, no longer stalling in your career. You are no longer a "doer" but a leader.

- Have more control over your destiny, and become a worthy example to friends, family, and your kids. You can chart the future on your terms, not on the terms of others.

But if you don't take the lessons in this book to heart:

- You may stay stuck where you are now.
- You will not be ready for new challenges.
- Your more politically savvy peers will continue to advance past you.
- You will lose critical time in what should be the prime of your career.
- You may get frustrated, derailed, and sidelined—and then you take that out on others.

I don't want you to get towards the end of a lackluster career and feel like you didn't give it your all, that you didn't take the risks that could have propelled you to the highest levels.

Follow the Rock, the Map and the Snowball to Get Real, Get Strategic, Get Doing—if you want to Get Promoted.

## Next Steps

But if it still feels daunting, or you set that trip wire—which indicates you are not getting ahead—then Get Help.

The ideas and concepts in this book are backed by decades of research and what I've seen personally coaching and helping thousands of executives implement these strategies.

But, as with anything, there are nuances of interpretation and ways in which your specific situation may require a slightly different approach. It's hard on your own, but not impossible, to get the perspective and identify the path and best steps quickly.

That's why a coach is so valuable. Coaching moves you from the research phase into action. You might be able to do this on your own, but sometimes you need a guide, an outside perspective, a coach who can be there challenging you, guiding you, helping keep you accountable, and most of all encouraging you.

Here's what happens when you work with me:

- You have a seasoned executive coach who will challenge, encourage, and help you develop recommendations based on what works (based on evidence and patterns I have seen with other executives), so you can get to your goals faster. I won't sugarcoat things. I'm direct and will challenge you in productive ways.
- You will be held accountable in biweekly sessions. You must move, and we'll make sure you maintain momentum.
- You will know I'm in your court and respecting your agenda.
- You will get resources, exercises, and tools tailored for your context, your working style, and business.
- You will have someone to unload on and speak to. You don't need to take this stuff home or to your boss at work (which is generally not a good idea).

- You will learn and develop habits and strategies that you can use for the rest of your career.
- We'll be in touch over time to help you identify opportunities, even after we stop working together.

I hope this book has helped you. There are additional resources listed that can help and many more on my website.

If you are ready to take your career to the next level and want to explore if I might be the right person to help you, then I suggest we set aside 30 minutes for a quick, friendly call.

By the end of that call, we'll both know if we're a fit for one another. No pressure either way.

To schedule your call, go to https://changwenderoth.com/apply/.

# ACKNOWLEDGMENTS

I want to thank three groups of people:

1) **The smart, hard-working, and selfless high-achieving executives** that I have had the privilege to coach and the many more I have spoken to or engaged with around the world.

   You challenged yourselves—often learning how to get out of your own way—to embrace and harness power and politics. You broke through to become more influential leaders in your organizations, communities, or fields. More importantly, you advanced towards your definitions of success, impact, and greater fulfillment. We need more of you in leadership positions. Coaching you through that journey has challenged me and made me, every year, an even better executive coach.

2) **To the academics, peers, and mentors** for their research, writing, feedback, and advice.

   There are too many academics to name, but you will see in the resources section those who have most influenced my thinking. As they say, "We stand on the shoulders of giants." However, there are two that I would like to call out specifically. First, Herminia Ibarra, for her work on leadership and working identity. The "Authenticity Paradox" sparked a critical "a-ha" moment that has helped me in infinite ways. Second, Jeff Pfeffer, whose views and work on the field of power, as well as feedback, encouragement and generosity of time, has been a touchstone for me. Jeff, your high-impact question and advice over dinner in Barcelona years back, well, that has made a tremendous difference. I'd also like to call out those who are able to unpack academic research, tell a memorable story and present break-through work that really shifts our thinking. Some reside in academia, but many do not: Dan Pink, Malcolm Gladwell, Adam Grant, Chip and Dan Health, Ron Friedman.

Among peers and mentors, I have found that Steve Jobs was indeed right when he said: "I've never found anybody who didn't want to help me when I've asked them for help." For me, reaching out and collaborating with others has been the biggest shift I've made from my younger days. To executive coaches Ed Batista, Paige Chen, and Agnes Le, for providing the initial encouragement and guidance when I started coaching. To Michael Melcher, for being my first executive coach years ago, an engagement that shifted how I saw coaching. And to Sharon Ruwart, whose pointed questions got me to move my ass in 2021. Thanks to those I have worked with at Stanford: Kevin Williams, for that short but powerful conversation in 2016 on taking risk; Inbal Demri for being an amazing collaborator and deep, thoughtful thinker; Lauren Capitani for always having amazing energy and insight; and Cecilia Hultén, Raquel Gonzalez-Dalmau, Jonathan Daves and Phil Mohabir. To the RExer community, particularly Dorie Clark, Rebecca Zucker, Ron Carucci, Nihar Chhaya, Susan Peppercorn, and Aviva Hirschfeld Legatt for paving inspiring paths and being generous with their pointed advice and encouragement. To my friends and colleagues at the Columbia University 3CP program. The 3CP certification draws from research, neuroscience, and adult learning. Thank you to Terrence E. Maltbia and the world-class team he has assembled.

To those who have encouraged me to write more and have taken time to edit and critique past articles (I am sure they are all happy I spared them being part of the editing process in this book): Kerry Parke at IE Business School, you rock. Felix Valdivieso, so glad you were among the first people I met at IE. To Tauna Szymanski, Leanna Herman, Peter Bai, Derek Briggs, Thao Le, for challenging me and making deeply insightful points—you guys operate on a different plane.

For the honor to work, speak, or share my ideas at big-name institutions: Key people who have helped me at my alma maters, Stanford University and Carleton College, and at IE Business School. Jenn Gardner, Megan Pearse, Marineh Lalikian in the Stanford LEAD program; John A Clendinin, Nacho Gafo, Joe Haslam, Kiron Ravindran, Carmen Abril, President Santiago

Iñiguez, Teresa Serra at IE; Marynel Ryan Van Zee, Rachel Leatham, Kimberly Betz (now running the Center for Career Development at Princeton) and RJ Reynolds at Carleton College. Returning to Carleton to speak, two times over a four-year span, was the spark that set this book in motion, and my visit there reminded me why Carleton is the #1 institution in the world in undergraduate teaching. To the late Roy Grow, and to Penny Prime, who first took me to China in 1992, showing what great teaching and experiential learning looked like.

To my former bosses, who kicked my ass in many ways (turns out fear is a bigger motivating force): Roberta Lipson, Bob Goodwin, Jason Shelton, David Thrower, Gil Laks, Luis Mora, Jose Ramón Pérez, Richard Twomey, Julie Tay and Ziya Muhamedcani. And lastly, to all the people who told me what was not possible and what "rules" we were supposed to follow. The chance to prove the naysayers wrong is a deeply motivating force. Margaret Mead's quote remains my touchstone: *"Never doubt that a small group of committed individuals can change the world. In fact, it's the only thing that ever has."*

3) **To my family:**
To my grandparents, on both sides, who modeled what hard work and perseverance should look like, left vivid childhood memories, and provided opportunities that got me where I am today. As the Chinese say, 吃水不忘挖井人, *"chi shui bu wang wa jing ren"* ("those that drink water should not forget who dug the well").

To my mom, whose leaning in, to my dad, whose listening and laying back, and to my brother, whose ability to forge his own path, have served as three very different models that I continue to draw from. Mom, I miss you deeply.

To my wife, Victoria, whose patience, support, and love has enabled all that we have, and the time for me to focus on coaching and writing this book.

And to Miguel 张明德 and Victoria 张明莉：Work hard, be curious, but above all: build your own power.

# RESOURCES (ENDNOTES)

[1] For the best overviews on power dynamics in organizations, see: 1) Pfeffer, J. (1992). *Managing with power: Politics and influence in organizations*. Harvard Business Press. 2) Hill, L. (1994). *Power Dynamics in Organizations*. Harvard Business Press. 3) Pfeffer, J. (2010). Power: *Why some people have it—and others don't*. New York, NY: HarperBusiness. 4) Battilana, Julie, and Tiziana Casciaro. *Power, for All: How It Really Works and Why It's Everyone's Business.* New York: Simon & Schuster, 2021. (Pfeffer's focuses more on power in organizations; Battilana and Casciaro's leans more to power in achieving societal change) 5) Caro, Robert A. (1974). *The Power Broker : Robert Moses and the fall of New York.* New York :Knopf. 6) Caro, R. A. (1983). *The Years of Lyndon Johnson*. New York: Vintage Books.

[2] Lerner, M. J., & Miller, D. T. (1978). Just world research and the attribution process: Looking back and ahead. *Psychological Bulletin, 85*(5), 1030–1051. https://doi.org/10.1037/0033-2909.85.5.1030

[3] Alvesson, M., & Einola, K. (2019). Warning for excessive positivity: Authentic leadership and other traps in leadership studies. *The Leadership Quarterly, 30*(4), 383-395. See also Pfeffer, J. (2015). *Leadership BS: Fixing workplaces and careers one truth at a time*. HarperCollins.

[4] Ibarra, H. (2015). The Authenticity Paradox. *Harvard Business Review, 93*(1/2), 53 59.

[5] Wenderoth, M. C. (2016). Great Leaders Embrace Office Politics. *Harvard Business Review*. https://hbr.org/2016/04/great-leaders-embrace-office-politics

[6] Foucault, M. (1991). *Discipline and Punish: The Birth of a Prison*. London, Penguin

7   Pfeffer, J. (2013). You're still the same: Why theories of power hold over time and across contexts. *Academy of Management Perspectives*, 27(4), 269-280.

8   Demri, I., & Wenderoth, M. (2021) Unpublished survey, conducted March 2021 with 240 global executives alumni of Stanford Business School Executive Education.

9   See: 1) Dobbin, F., & Kalev, A. (2016). Why diversity programs fail. *Harvard Business Review*, 94(7), 14. 2) Kalev, A., & Dobbin, F. (2020). Companies need to think bigger than diversity training. *Harvard Business Review Digital Articles*.

10   For more on the "Better than average effect": Zell, E., Strickhouser, J. E., Sedikides, C., & Alicke, M. D. (2020). The better-than-average effect in comparative self-evaluation: A comprehensive review and meta-analysis. *Psychological Bulletin*, 146(2), 118.

11   See 1) Dweck, C. S. (2008). *Mindset: The new psychology of success*. Random House Digital, Inc.. 2) Duckworth, A. (2016). *Grit: The power of passion and perseverance*. New York, NY: Scribner.

12   Grant, A. M. (2013). *Give and take: A revolutionary approach to success*. Penguin.

13   For an overview on why this works, and why constraints and limits get us to more creative solutions, read: Wenderoth, M. (2020) *The Constraints That Move Us Forward: How Covid-19 Has Sparked Creative Solutions*. Forbes. https://www.forbes. com/sites/michaelcwenderoth/2020/05/15/the-constraints- that-move-us-forward-how-covid-19-has-sparked-creative- solutions/?sh=5eb190d97237. For other excellent resources on creativity and innovation: 1) Seelig, T. (2012). *inGenius: A crash course on creativity*. Hay House, Inc., 2) De Bono, E., & Zimbalist, E. (1970). *Lateral thinking* (pp. 1-32). London: Penguin. 3) Varol, O. (2020). *Think Like a Rocket Scientist: Simple Strategies for Giant Leaps in Work and Life*. Random House., 4) Brown, T. (2008). Design thinking. *Harvard business review*, 86(6), 84. 5) IDEO offers excellent "method cards" here: https://www.designkit.org/methods

14   Edmondson, A. C. (2018). *The fearless organization: Creating psychological safety in the workplace for learning, innovation, and growth*. John Wiley & Sons.

[15]  Kramer, R. M. (2009). Rethinking trust. *Harvard Business Review*, 87(6), 68-77.

[16]  For solid academic overviews on power in organizations, see: 1) Pfeffer, J. (1992). *Managing with Power: Politics and influence in organizations*. Harvard Business Press. 2) Hill, L. (1994). *Power Dynamics in Organizations.* Harvard Business Press.

[17]  Ferris, G. R., Treadway, D. C., Kolodinsky, R. W., Hochwarter, W. A., Kacmar, C. J., Douglas, C., & Frink, D. D. (2005). Development and validation of the political skill inventory. *Journal of management*, 31(1), 126-152.

[18]  Ahearn, K. K., Ferris, G. R., Hochwarter, W. A., Douglas, C., & Ammeter, A. P. (2004). Leader political skill and team performance. *Journal of management*, 30(3), 309-327.

[19]  Goleman, D. (2012). *Emotional intelligence: Why it can matter more than IQ*. Bantam.

[20]  Goleman, D. (2017). *What Makes a Leader?(Harvard Business Review Classics)*. Harvard Business Press.

[21]  Templer, K. J. (2018). Dark personality, job performance ratings, and the role of political skill: An indication of why toxic people may get ahead at work. *Personality and Individual Differences*, 124, 209-214.

[22]  Templer, K. J. (2018)  Why Do Toxic People Get Promoted? For the Same Reason Humble People Do: Political Skill. *Harvard Business Review.*

[23]  Cialdini, R. B. (1987). *Influence* (Vol. 3). Port Harcourt: A. Michel.

[24]  See, for example: Burkett, R. An Alternate Framework for Agent Recruitment: From MICE to RASCLS. *Studies in Intelligence* Vol. 57, No. 1 (Extracts, March 2013) https://cyberwar.nl/d/fromCIA.gov/Burkett-MICE%20to%20 RASCALS.pdf Note that this is more or less Robert Cialdini's 6 principles, with a different "RASCLS" acronym.

[25]  Ariely, D., & Jones, S. (2008). *Predictably Irrational*. New York, NY: Harper.

[26]  Kahneman, D. (2011). *Thinking, Fast and Slow*. Macmillan.

[27] Kramer, R. M. (2006). The great intimidators. *Harvard Business Review*, *84*(2), 88-96.

[28] Kahneman, D., Knetsch, J. L., & Thaler, R. H. (1991). Anomalies: The endowment effect, loss aversion, and status quo bias. *Journal of Economic perspectives*, *5*(1), 193-206.

[29] Wolff, H. G., & Moser, K. (2009). Effects of networking on career success: a longitudinal study. *Journal of Applied Psychology*, *94*(1), 196.

[30] Granovetter, M. S. (1973). The strength of weak ties. *American journal of sociology*, *78*(6), 1360-1380.

[31] Epstein, D. (2021). *Range: Why generalists triumph in a specialized world*. Penguin.

[32] Burt, R. S. (1992). *Structural holes*. Harvard university press.

[33] Burt, R. S. (2004). Structural holes and good ideas. *American journal of sociology*, *110*(2), 349-399.

[34] Burt, R. S. (2000). The network structure of social capital. *Research in organizational behavior*, *22*, 345-423.

[35] Burt, R. S., Hogarth, R. M., & Michaud, C. (2000). The social capital of French and American managers. *Organization science*, *11*(2), 123-147.

[36] Burt, R. S., & Ronchi, D. (2007). Teaching executives to see social capital: Results from a field experiment. *Social Science Research*, *36*(3), 1156-1183.

[37] Albert-Laszlo Barabasi. (2018). The Formula: The Universal Laws of Success, New York, NY: Little, Brown, and Company.

[38] Ibarra, H., Carter, N. M., & Silva, C. (2010). Why men still get more promotions than women. *Harvard business review*, *88*(9), 80-85.

[39] Hewlett, S. A. (2013). *Forget a mentor, find a sponsor: The new way to fast-track your career*. Harvard Business Review Press.

[40] See, for example 1) Foust-Cummings, H. & Dinolfo, S. and Kohler, J. (2011) Sponsoring Women To Success. *Catalyst*. https://www.catalyst.org/wp-content/uploads/2019/01/sponsoring_women_to_success.pdf 2) McKinsey's annual Women in the Workplace reports, which

have covered this topic for numerous years. The 2021 issue: https://www.mckinsey.com/featured-insights/diversity-and-inclusion/women-in-the-workplace

[41] Yang, Yang, Nitesh V. Chawla, and Brian Uzzi. "A network's gender composition and communication pattern predict women's leadership success." *Proceedings of the National Academy of Sciences* 116, no. 6 (2019): 2033-2038.

[42] Ibarra, H. (2015) How to Revive a Tired Network. *Harvard Business Review.*

[43] Clark, D. (2015). *Stand out: How to find your breakthrough idea and build a following around it.* Penguin.

[44] Wilson, T. D., & Schooler, J. W. (1991). Thinking too much: introspection can reduce the quality of preferences and decisions. *Journal of personality and social psychology*, 60(2), 181.

[45] Pfeffer, J., Fong, C. T., Cialdini, R. B., & Portnoy, R. R. (2006). Overcoming the self-promotion dilemma: Interpersonal attraction and extra help as a consequence of who sings one's praises. *Personality and Social Psychology Bulletin*, 32(10), 1362-1374.

[46] Bornstein, R. F. (1989). Exposure and affect: overview and meta-analysis of research, 1968–1987. *Psychological bulletin*, 106(2), 265.

[47] Trout, J., & Ries, A. (1986). *Positioning: The battle for your mind.* New York, NY: McGraw-Hill.

[48] Hewlett, S. A., & Ashford, R. (2014). *Executive presence.* HarperCollins.

[49] Willis, J., & Todorov, A. (2006). First impressions: Making up your mind after a 100-ms exposure to a face. *Psychological science*, 17(7), 592-598.

[50] Friedman, Vanessa. (2021) "Everything About You Must Say Power." *New York Times.* https://www.nytimes.com/2021/11/03/style/eric-adams-style.html

[51] Cialdini, R. (2016). *Pre-suasion: A revolutionary way to influence and persuade.* Simon and Schuster.

52 Albert Mehrabian's work is often misinterpreted and misquoted. For a quick review see:Thompson, J. (2011) Is Nonverbal Communication a Numbers Game? *Psychology Today.* https://www.psychologytoday.com/us/blog/beyond-words/201109/is-nonverbal-communication-numbers-game

53 Heath, C., & Heath, D. (2007). *Made to stick: Why some ideas survive and others die.* Random House.

54 Abrahams, M. (2015) Tips and Techniques for More Confident and Compelling Presentations. *Stanford Business Insights.* https://www.gsb.stanford.edu/insights/matt-abrahams-tips-techniques-more-confident-compelling-presentations

55 Tannen, D. (1995). The power of talk: Who gets heard and why. *Harvard Business Review,* 73(5), 138-148.

56 Battilana, J., & Casciaro, T. (2021). *Power, for All: How It Really Works and Why It's Everyone's Business.* Simon and Schuster, p. 73 (iBook version).

57 See: 1) Mayo, M. (2017). If humble people make the best leaders, why do we fall for charismatic narcissists. *Harvard Bus. Rev, 4,* 2-5. 2) Chamorro-Premuzic, T. (2013). Why do so many incompetent men become leaders. *Harvard Business Review, 22.*

58 Antonakis, J., Fenley, M., & Liechti, S. (2011). Can charisma be taught? Tests of two interventions. *Academy of Management Learning & Education, 10*(3), 374-396.

59 Rubin, Harriet. (2007) Shall I Compare Thee to an Andy Grove? *Strategy + Business.* https://www.strategy-business.com/article/07402

60 Lammers, J., Dubois, D., Rucker, D. D., & Galinsky, A. D. (2013). Power gets the job: Priming power improves interview outcomes. *Journal of Experimental Social Psychology, 49*(4), 776-779.

61 Galinsky, A. D., Gruenfeld, D. H., & Magee, J. C. (2003). From power to action. *Journal of personality and social psychology, 85*(3), 453.

62 Carney, D. R., Cuddy, A. J., & Yap, A. J. (2010). Power posing: Brief nonverbal displays affect neuroendocrine levels and risk tolerance. *Psychological science, 21*(10), 1363-1368.

[63] Galinsky, A. D., Magee, J. C., Inesi, M. E., & Gruenfeld, D. H. (2006). Power and perspectives not taken. *Psychological science*, 17(12), 1068-1074.

[64] Gruenfeld, D. (2020). *Acting with Power.* New York: Currency/Penguin Random House.

[65] Batista, E. (2021). Force Isn't Power. *Personal Blog.* https://www.edbatista.com/2021/03/force-isnt-power.html

[66] De Mesquita, B. B., & Smith, A. (2011). *The dictator's handbook: why bad behavior is almost always good politics.* PublicAffairs.

[67] McClelland, D. C., & Burnham, D. H. (2008). *Power is the great motivator.* Harvard Business Review Press.

[68] Pfeffer, J. (2010). Power: *Why some people have it--and others don't.* New York, NY: HarperBusiness.

[69] Tiedens, L. Z., Ellsworth, P. C., & Mesquita, B. (2000). Sentimental stereotypes: Emotional expectations for high-and low-status group members. *Personality and Social Psychology Bulletin*, 26(5), 560-575.

[70] Tiedens, L. Z. (2001). Anger and advancement versus sadness and subjugation: the effect of negative emotion expressions on social status conferral. *Journal of personality and social psychology*, 80(1), 86.

[71] See Key & Peele - Obama's Anger Translator - Meet Luther—Uncensored: https://www.youtube.com/watch?v=-qv7k2_lc0M

[72] Gaertig, C., Barasch, A., Levine, E. E., & Schweitzer, M. E. (2019). When does anger boost status?. *Journal of Experimental Social Psychology*, 85, 103876.

[73] Wenderoth, M. (2020) Why Channeling Anger Can Be A Leadership Strength. *Forbes.* https://www.forbes.com/sites/michaelcwenderoth/2020/06/16/why-channeling-anger-can-be-a-leadership-strength/?sh=6a88502c7e15

[74] De Cremer, D., Pillutla, M. M., & Folmer, C. R. (2011). How important is an apology to you? Forecasting errors in evaluating the value of apologies. *Psychological Science*, 22(1), 45-48.

[75] Sunstein, C. (2019) In Politics, Apologies Are for Losers: At least that's what the numbers say. *New York Times.* https://www.nytimes.

com/2019/07/27/opinion/sunday/when-should-a-politician-apologize.
html

76    Pfeffer, J. (2015) Corporate apologies: Beware the pitfalls
      of saying sorry. *Fortune*. https://fortune.com/2015/10/26/
      corporate-apologies-crisis-management/

77    Brescoll, V. L., & Uhlmann, E. L. (2008). Can an angry woman get
      ahead? Status conferral, gender, and expression of emotion in the
      workplace. *Psychological science*, *19*(3), 268-275.

78    Gee, B. & Peck, D. (2015) The Illusion of Asian Success. *Ascend*.
      https://ascendleadership.site-ym.com/page/Research

79    Berdahl, J. L., & Min, J. A. (2012). Prescriptive stereotypes and
      workplace consequences for East Asians in North America. *Cultural
      Diversity and Ethnic Minority Psychology*, *18*(2), 141.

80    See: 1) Livingston, R. W., & Pearce, N. A. (2009). The teddy-bear
      effect: Does having a baby face benefit black chief executive
      officers? *Psychological science*, *20*(10), 1229-1236. 2) Livingston, R.
      W., Rosette, A. S., & Washington, E. F. (2012). Can an agentic Black
      woman get ahead? The impact of race and interpersonal dominance
      on perceptions of female leaders. *Psychological science*, *23*(4), 354-358.

81    References: 1) Pfeffer, J. (2013). You're still the same: Why theories of
      power hold over time and across contexts. *Academy of Management
      Perspectives*, *27*(4), 269-280. 2) Cialdini, R. B. (1993). The psychology
      of persuasion. *New York*.; Burt, R. S. (2004). Structural holes and
      good ideas. *American journal of sociology*, *110*(2), 349-399.; Chen,
      H., Jiang, S., & Wu, M. (2021). How important are political skills
      for career success? A systematic review and meta-analysis. The
      International Journal of Human Resource Management, 1-27.
      3) Carney, D. R., Hall, J. A., & LeBeau, L. S. (2005). Beliefs about
      the nonverbal expression of social power. *Journal of Nonverbal
      Behavior*, *29*(2), 105-123. 4) Galinsky, A., & Schweitzer, M.
      (2015). *Friend & foe: When to cooperate, when to compete, and how to
      succeed at both*. Currency. Chapter 2.

82    Ely, R. J., Ibarra, H., & Kolb, D. M. (2011). Taking gender into
      account: Theory and design for women's leadership development
      programs. *Academy of Management Learning & Education*, *10*(3),
      474-493.

[83] Private but unpublished speeches on women and power by Inbal Demri at Stanford University (2018-2022). See www.inbaldemri.com.

[84] For the best resources on understanding and managing cultural differences in organizations: 1) Gelfand, M. (2019). *Rule makers, rule breakers: Tight and loose cultures and the secret signals that direct our lives*. Scribner. 2) Hofstede, G. (2011). Dimensionalizing cultures: The Hofstede model in context. *Online readings in psychology and culture*, 2(1), 2307-0919. 3) Meyer, E. (2014). *The Culture Map: Breaking through the invisible boundaries of global business*. Public Affairs. 4) The idea of "cultural intelligence": Ang, S., Van Dyne, L., Koh, C., Ng, K. Y., Templer, K. J., Tay, C., & Chandrasekar, N. A. (2007). Cultural intelligence: Its measurement and effects on cultural judgment and decision making, cultural adaptation and task performance. *Management and organization review*, 3(3), 335-371. 5) Finally, see also Gabor Holch's excellent overview of what cross-culture leadership is — and is not: https://www.talentmgt.com/articles/2018/05/10/cross-cultural-leadership-skills-not-think/

[85] Williams, J. C., & Dempsey, R. (2014). *What Works for Women at Work*. New York University Press.

[86] Private but unpublished speeches on women and power by Inbal Demri at Stanford University (2018-2022). See www.inbaldemri.com.

[87] Sandberg, S. (2013). *Lean in: Women, Work, and the Will to Lead*. Random House.

[88] Wenderoth, M. (2018) Manage Your Career Like a Top Sales Rep. *Forbes*. https://www.forbesindia.com/article/ie/manage-your-career-like-a-top-sales-rep/48955/1

[89] Flynn, F. J., & Lake, V. K. (2008). If you need help, just ask: Underestimating compliance with direct requests for help. *Journal of personality and social psychology*, 95(1), 128.

[90] Langer, E. J., Blank, A., & Chanowitz, B. (1978). The mindlessness of ostensibly thoughtful action: The role of" placebic" information in interpersonal interaction. *Journal of personality and social psychology*, 36(6), 635.

[91] See for example: 1) Neale, M. A., & Lys, T. Z. (2015). *Getting (more of) what you want: How the secrets of economics and psychology can help you negotiate anything, in business and in life*. Basic Books. 2)

Watkins, M., & Rosegrant, S. (1996). Sources of power in coalition building. *Negotiation journal*, *12*(1), 47-68.

[92] Wenderoth, M. (2019). How to Strengthen Work Relationships and Advance Your Career. *Harvard Business Review*. https://changwenderoth.com/wp-content/uploads/2021/08/how-to-strengthen-work-relationships-and-advance-your-career-hbr-ascend.pdf

[93] Galinsky, A. D., Maddux, W. W., Gilin, D., & White, J. B. (2008). Why it pays to get inside the head of your opponent: The differential effects of perspective taking and empathy in negotiations. *Psychological science*, *19*(4), 378-384.

[94] Berg, J. M., Dutton, J. E., & Wrzesniewski, A. (2008). What is job crafting and why does it matter? *Retrieved from the website of Positive Organizational Scholarship on April*, *15*, 2011.

[95] Wenderoth, M. (2019) Why You're Professional Networking Isn't Working. *Harvard Business Review*. https://changwenderoth.com/wp-content/uploads/2021/08/why-your-professional-networking-isnt-working-hbr-ascend.pdf

[96] Top resources on habit formation and behavioral change: 1) Fogg, B. J. (2019). *Tiny habits: the small changes that change everything*. Eamon Dolan Books. 2) Dean, J. (2013). *Making habits, breaking habits: How to make changes that stick*. Simon and Schuster., 3) McGonigal, K. (2013). *The willpower instinct: How self-control works, why it matters, and what you can do to get more of it*. Penguin. 4) Milkman, K., & Milkman, K. L. (2021). *How to Change: The Science of Getting from Where You Are to Where You Want to Be*. Penguin. 5) Duhigg, C. (2012). *The power of habit: Why we do what we do in life and business*. Random House. 6) Heath, C., & Heath, D. (2011). *Switch*. 7) The articles of Jason Hreha, which puts behavioral science in perspective, https://www.thebehavioralscientist.com/articles.

[97] Setting goals and keeping score are incredibly important to advancement. For an excellent overview on ways to keep track—and not keep track, see: Friedman, R. (2021) *Decoding Greatness*. Simon and Schuster. Chapter 4.

[98] Ferrazzi, K., & Raz, T. (2005). *Never Eat Alone: And Other Secrets to Success. One Relationship at a Time*.

[99] Casciaro, T., Gino, F., & Kouchaki, M. (2016). Learn to love networking: Interaction. *Harvard Business Review*, *94*(7), 4.

[100] Fast, N. J., Gruenfeld, D. H., Sivanathan, N., & Galinsky, A. D. (2009). Illusory control: A generative force behind power's far-reaching effects. *Psychological Science*, *20*(4), 502-508.

[101] Keltner, D., Gruenfeld, D. H., & Anderson, C. (2003). Power, approach, and inhibition. *Psychological review*, *110*(2), 265.

[102] Magee, J. C., & Galinsky, A. D. (2008). 8 social hierarchy: The self-reinforcing nature of power and status. *Academy of Management annals*, *2*(1), 351-398.

[103] Chatterjee, A., & Hambrick, D. C. (2007). It's all about me: Narcissistic chief executive officers and their effects on company strategy and performance. *Administrative science quarterly*, *52*(3), 351-386.

[104] Carucci, Ron. (2015) 4 Ways Leaders Fritter Their Power Away. *Harvard Business Review*.

[105] Seligman, M. E., & Csikszentmihalyi, M. (2014). Positive psychology: An introduction. In *Flow and the foundations of positive psychology* (pp. 279-298). Springer, Dordrecht.

Printed in Great Britain
by Amazon

46397049R00169